200 ten-minute meals

hamlyn | all colour cookbook

200 ten-minute meals

Denise Smart

An Hachette UK Company
www.hachette.co.uk

First published in Great Britain in 2013 by Hamlyn
a division of Octopus Publishing Group Ltd
Endeavour House, 189 Shaftesbury Avenue
London WC2H 8JY
www.octopusbooks.co.uk

ISBN: 978-0-600-62529-2

A CIP catalogue record for this book is available from the
British Library

Printed and bound in China

10 9 8 7 6 5 4 3 2 1

Both metric and imperial measurements have been
given in all recipes. Use one set of measurements only,
and not a mixture of both.

Standard level spoon measurements are used in all recipes
1 tablespoon = 15 ml spoon
1 teaspoon = 5 ml spoon

Ovens should be preheated to the specified temperature –
if using a fan-assisted oven, follow the manufacturer's
instructions for adjusting the time and temperature.

Fresh herbs should be used unless otherwise stated.
Medium eggs should be used unless otherwise stated.

This book includes dishes made with nuts and nut
derivatives. It is advisable for those with known allergic
reactions to nuts and nut derivatives to avoid dishes made
with these. It is prudent to check the labels of all pre-
prepared ingredients for the possible inclusion of nut
derivatives. Vulnerable people, such as pregnant and
nursing mothers, invalids, the elderly, babies and young
children, should avoid dishes containg raw or lightlly
cooked eggs.

Some of the recipes in this book have previously appeared
in other titles published by Hamlyn.

contents

introduction

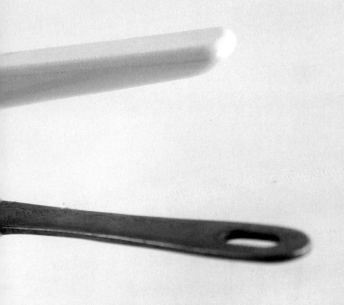

introduction

Can you really cook a delicious meal in only 10 minutes? Yes, you can! All it takes is a little bit of forward planning, a well-stocked refrigerator, freezer and storecupboard, and a little help from your supermarket, fishmonger and butcher.

In the time it would take you to pick up the telephone and order a takeaway, or prick the plastic film on a ready meal and wait for it to heat up in microwave, you could have made a much more delicious and nutritious dinner from scratch.

If you've had a long day, the car broke down, the train was delayed, you've been stuck in traffic trying to get home or had to work late, the last thing you want to

do is think about planning, shopping for and cooking a meal. But follow these few simple guidelines and you will be able to put together a tasty, wholesome meal in a matter of minutes.

Take a little time out and do a weekly meal plan so you know what you are going to cook and can organize your shopping accordingly, thus making sure you have everything to hand and can avoid waste. Why not make use of internet shopping? Once you have done this once, ordering your groceries becomes quicker and easier on subsequent orders. The food is delivered to you at your convenience and is packed into sections, so it is easy to put away. This alone could save you hours each month.

ingredients

To make food taste delicious in double-quick time, you will need to add lots of flavoursome ingredients that will have an instant impact on your dish, so make sure to stock up on your favourite pastes, herbs, spices and sauces.

You can also try keeping pots of growing herbs on your windowledge – apart from looking attractive, they will ensure you have a supply of fresh herbs to hand that will liven up a variety of recipes. Just remember to water them from time to time!

Jars of ready-chopped or minced ginger, garlic and lemon grass are marvelous time-savers and will reduce your preparation time hugely. Meat and fish can be bought ready-trimmed and cut into chunks or strips. Not only will you be saved the preparation time, but these small pieces cook very quickly too. Many vegetables can also be bought ready-peeled and chopped, again saving valuable minutes in the kitchen at the end of a long, busy day.

Cooking a meal in just 10 minutes inevitably involves the clever use of pre-prepared ingredients. You can find all the items that are used in these recipes in major supermarkets. Below is a list of the more commonly used ingredients in this book, ingredients which it is helpful to keep ready-to-hand in your storecupboard, refrigerator and freezer.

the storecupboard

The most useful source of quick meals is probably the storecupboard. After reading through the recipes in this book, you will soon be able to create some quick culinary masterpieces of your own, even if you haven't organized or planned to cook a specific dish.

Remember to keep a list of the items you have used, so you can restock next time you go shopping. Organize your storecupboard so that things are always easy to find and remember that once some items, such as jars of pastes or coconut milk, are opened, they need to be stored in the refrigerator to keep them fresh.

storecupboard essentials
canned foods
- chopped tomatoes
- pulses, such as chickpeas, Puy lentils and butter beans
- vegetables and fruit, such as sweetcorn and pineapple
- fish, such as salmon and tuna, in brine or water, as well as anchovy fillets
- coconut milk

jars & bottles

- tomato purée and ketchup
- Worcestershire sauce
- curry pastes and harissa
- sweet chilli sauce
- dark soy sauce
- English, French and wholegrain mustards
- Thai fish sauce
- wasabi paste
- mango chutney and caramelized onions
- a selection of oils, such as sunflower, olive and sesame oil
- a selection of vinegars, such as balsamic and white wine vinegar

sweet things

- honey and maple syrup
- ready-made fruit coulis and chocolate sauce
- extracts such as vanilla, peppermint and orange
- caster sugar and soft brown sugar
- ready-made pastry cases and meringues

herbs, spices & flavourings

- ready-chopped or minced garlic, ginger and lemon grass
- dried herbs, such as thyme and mint
- spices, such as Cajun seasoning, chilli powder, paprika, cinnamon and curry powder
- salt and pepper
- good-quality stock cubes
- good-quality gravy granules

dry ingredients

- plain flour and cornflour
- quick-cooking types of dried pasta, such as angel hair and orzo
- couscous
- ready-cooked rice, vacuum-packed in sachets
- ready-cooked egg noodles and rice noodles, vacuum-packed in sachets
- chopped cashews, peanuts and pecans
- sesame seeds

11

the refrigerator

Fresh produce, such as meat, fish and seafood, should be bought as fresh as possible and with specific meals in mind to reduce wastage. If timing allows, it's best to buy them on the day you're planning to cook them if you can.

It is also a good idea to get to know your local butcher and fishmonger; this way you can get them to do a lot of the preparation for you, so saving you time in the kitchen later. Otherwise make use of the butchers and fishmongers to be found in the larger supermarkets.

refrigerator essentials
- bags of prepared salad leaves, such as rocket, watercress and baby spinach
- packs of ready-chopped stir-fry vegetables and beansprouts
- packs of ready-chopped onions and sliced mushrooms
- fresh vegetables, such as red peppers, new potatoes, spring onions and carrots
- ready-diced or chopped pancetta and chorizo
- sliced cooked meats, such as chicken and ham
- fresh breadcrumbs
- fresh pasta and gnocchi
- fresh ready-made mashed potatoes
- ready-grated Parmesan and Cheddar cheese
- yogurt, such as Greek and natural
- butter
- eggs
- double cream, crème fraîche and soured cream
- tubs of fresh cheese sauce, tomato sauce and pesto
- tubs of ready-made fresh tomato salsa and guacamole

the freezer

This really is a much under-used piece of kitchen equipment nowadays, not only for storing foods that are bought frozen but also for storing foods that you prepare and freeze yourself.

Frozen food is frequently thought of as inferior to fresh produce, but the opposite is often true: frozen vegetables such as peas contain more vitamins than fresh peas as they are frozen just after picking, when they are at their very best. Freezing also allows you to enjoy your favourite fruits and vegetables whenever you like, whether they are in season or not.

Frozen meat is not only just as nutritious as fresh, it is often cheaper. In many ways, frozen fish and seafood are even better than fresh: when fish is frozen at sea as soon as it is caught, all the taste and goodness is locked in. And it is often better for the environment, too, as frozen fish does not have to be air-freighted but can be transported by ship or overland. For best results, thaw frozen seafood or meat by placing it in the refrigerator overnight. Once it has thawed, do not refreeze it, but treat it as you would fresh produce.

Frozen food will of course also keep for much longer than fresh, and you can reduce food waste by only thawing and using the amount you need for each meal. Bread keeps well in the freezer, so freeze pittas, naan breads and halved muffins so you always have a useful supply to hand.

If you are organized enough and have a few minutes to spare, you can make your own breadcrumbs from slightly stale bread – the food processor makes light work of this task – and freeze them for use later.

You can also freeze your own grated ginger and chopped garlic, or grate some Cheddar and Parmesan cheese and freeze it in small containers for meals later in the week.

When cooking rice as an accompaniment, cook extra quantities to freeze in portions. Try cooking a double quantity of some dishes, such as Creamy Paprika Chicken (see page 124) or Thai Massaman Chicken Curry (see page 114), so you can freeze half to create your own ready meal.

- bread, such as naan, pitta and sliced white
- ice cream
- bags of berries, such as raspberries, blueberries and mixed berries
- squid rings and prawns (remember to defrost them in the refrigerator)
- ready-rolled puff pastry

equipment

Do not underestimate how vitally important good tools are to speed up the cooking process. To prepare a quick and simple meal, all you need are a few good-quality items of kitchen equipment.

- A large, heavy-based frying pan or wok. This is essential for many of the quick-cook recipes in this book. A thick base spreads the heat evenly, allowing you to cook at high temperatures without burning. A heatproof or detachable handle is a useful feature so you can continue cooking under the grill or in the oven.
- A selection of good-quality saucepans with lids, a ridged griddle pan, a large colander and a sieve are also essential.
- Good knives are vital. You will need at least two: a small knife for paring and slicing, and a larger one for chopping. Remember that a sharp knife will enable you to work more quickly and is safer than a blunt one.
- Basic utensils, such as spoons for stirring, a fish slice, a slotted spoon, vegetable peeler, balloon whisk and a pair of tongs are also needed.

freezer essentials
- bags of mixed vegetables, such as Mediterranean vegetables
- bags of peas
- tubs of chopped chilli, garlic and ginger
- tubs of chopped herbs, such as parsley and coriander

14

- A grater is another invaluable tool. Choose one that is comfortable to hold, has a range of different blades and is sharp. Microplanes are fantastic for quickly removing the rind from citrus fruits.
- Make sure you have at least two baking sheets, a selection of bowls of different sizes for mixing and a measuring jug.
- Don't forget a set of scales and measuring spoons for the accurate measurement of ingredients.
- You will also need a few chopping boards, so that you can keep one for preparing vegetables and fruit and separate chopping boards for meat and fish.

electric appliances

Some electrical equipment can also help you save time. Buy a good-quality food processor to make quick work of whizzing up pastes and pestos, blending soups and chopping fruits and nuts. An electric hand-held whisk is another great time-saving device, allowing you to whisk eggs and cream in no time. Lastly, a microwave has many uses apart from reheating ready meals. Use it to melt chocolate, defrost frozen foods, reheat ready-made mashed potatoes and cook vegetables to serve with some of your 10-minute meals.

quick cooking methods

Most recipes in this book use one of the following quick cook methods. Follow the tips below for guaranteed success.

Stir-frying You will need a wok or a large, deep frying pan. Preheat the pan until hot, then add the oil. Make sure the oil is very hot before adding the ingredients, as this will ensure the food is sealed quickly on the outside to retain all its juices and brown nicely to develop maximum flavour. Cut meat and vegetables into even-sized pieces so they all cook at the same rate.

Deep fat frying You can use a wok or deep saucepan if you don't have a deep fat fryer. Make sure the oil is hot enough before

adding the food: use a thermometer to check the temperature or drop a cube of bread into the oil; when the bread turns golden in 15 seconds, the oil has reached the correct temperature. If the temperature of the oil is too low, the food will be soggy and absorb a lot of oil. If you are using a deep fat fryer, you can set the dial to the correct temperature.

Grilling Make sure the grill is preheated to high before placing the food under it. Place the food as near to the element as possible, without it touching.

Griddling When griddling, lightly oil the food on both sides before adding it to the pan. Preheat the griddle pan until very hot before adding the food. If you need to oil the pan, dip a sheet of kitchen paper in a little oil, rub it over the surface of the pan, preheat the pan and when it is smoking, add the food.

tips for organizing your kitchen

Make your kitchen works for you, so you can find things quickly. Next time you have a spare hour, reorganize your kitchen to make it easier to work in.

- It may sound obvious, but place frequently used utensils such as wooden spoons, tongs and fish slices next to the cooker in a jug or pot, or hanging from a rail, so they are close to hand when you need them.
- Reorganize your cutlery and utensils drawer so that items you use most are at the front. Keep knives in a knife block or

rack on top of the worktop, not stuck at the back of a drawer where they will become blunt and are likely to cut you.

- Don't hide the food processor and hand-held whisk at the back of a cupboard or behind heavy equipment so they are hard to reach and too much bother to use.
- Keep mixing bowls and measuring jugs together, baking trays in a drawer under or close to the cooker and ovenproof dishes in an easy-to-reach place.
- Keep your work surface free from clutter, so you have plenty of space to work. A tidy kitchen will make you feel more organized

and this, in turn, will allow you to work faster and more efficiently.

complete your meal

It is all very well cooking a recipe in a matter of minutes, but how do you turn that into a well-balanced and satisfying meal? If a dish can be cooked in 10 minutes, you don't want to spend any more time than necessary making an accompaniment to serve with it.

Ready-made mashed potatoes bought from the chiller cabinet in the supermarket and sachets of ready-cooked noodles and rice make great accompaniments to a variety of dishes and take just a few minutes to reheat. And don't forget bread as a nutritious, satisfying and quick accompaniment, from soft naan breads or toasted chapattis with a curry to crusty bread with a bowl of soup. However, if a dish already contains a carbohydrate, such as rice, pasta or potatoes, serve it with some green salad or an additional portion of vegetables instead.

Frozen vegetables, such as frozen leaf spinach and peas, are very quick to cook, especially in the microwave. Most supermarkets stock a good range of ready-prepared fresh vegetables, such as mangetout, sugar snaps, asparagus and fine beans which take a matter of minutes to cook in a saucepan of salted boiling water while you are cooking your main dish. And

ready-prepared leaves, tomatoes, cucumber and other raw ingredients are very quickly assembled into a vitamin-packed salad.

how to follow the recipes

- Before you start cooking, ensure you have all the ingredients to hand as well as the right cooking utensils and equipment.
- Always read right through the recipe first, so you know what is ahead. You may need to preheat a grill or oven, or heat oil in a wok or deep fat fryer.
- You will need to learn the art of multi-tasking; while something is cooking in one pan, you may need to be stirring something else in another pan. Once you've done this a few times, you will find it gets easier and you will get quicker!
- Take the recipes one step at a time, following the steps in order. You will need to prepare or chop the next ingredients as you go along, while you are waiting for other ingredients to cook, rather than doing all the preparation at the beginning. This will ensure you complete the recipes in 10 minutes.
- Ensure stock is hot by dissolving stock cubes in boiling water and always use boiling water from a kettle to fill a saucepan for cooking vegetables, pasta and rice. This will help keep the cooking times within 10 minutes.
- While you are cooking, get other members of the household to lay the table for you.

Getting children involved in some stage of the procedure, whether it is helping to stir the food or laying the table, will encourage happy mealtimes.

- Don't get stressed! It will slow you down and ruin what should be an enjoyable experience. If a recipe takes you 12 minutes rather than 10, don't worry. We all work at different rates and some people will be able to chop quicker than others.
- Finally, have fun: enjoy the aromas and the success of a quick and delicious meal coming together.

snacks & light meals

tuna quesadilla with salsa

Serves **2**
Preparation time **4 minutes**
Cooking time **4–6 minutes**

2 **soft flour tortillas**
4 tablespoons **ready-made
fresh tomato salsa**
2 **spring onions**, roughly
chopped
75 g (3 oz) **canned tuna**,
drained
50 g (2 oz) **canned
sweetcorn with peppers**,
drained
75 g (3 oz) **mozzarella
cheese**, grated
olive oil, for brushing

Place 1 tortilla on a plate and spread with the salsa.
Sprinkle with the spring onions, tuna, sweetcorn and
cheese. Place the second tortilla on top and press down.

Heat a large frying pan and brush with oil. Place the
quesadilla in the pan and cook over a moderate heat
for 2–3 minutes, pressing down with a spatula until the
cheese starts to melt.

Place an inverted plate over the pan and turn the pan
and plate together to tip the quesadilla on to the plate.
Slide back into the pan and cook the other side for 2–3
minutes. Remove from the pan and cut into wedges.

For prosciutto tortilla pizzas, place 2 soft flour
tortillas on a large baking sheet and spread with
4 tablespoons ready-made pizza sauce. Arrange
4 chopped slices of proscuitto and 125 g (4 oz) sliced
mozzarella on top. Cook under a preheated hot grill
for 2–3 minutes until the cheese has melted. Serve
immediately with a large handful of rocket leaves
scattered over the top and a drizzle of olive oil.

haloumi, orange & mint salad

Serves **2**
Preparation time **6 minutes**
Cooking time **2–4 minutes**

2 **oranges,** peeled
4 tablespoons **chopped mint**
2 teaspoons **white wine
  vinegar**
2 tablespoons **olive oil**
1 teaspoon **honey**
50 g (2 oz) **pine nuts**
250 g (8 oz) **haloumi cheese,**
  cut into 8–10 slices
125 g (4 oz) **prepared
  watercress** and baby
  spinach
salt and **pepper**

Divide the oranges into segments by cutting between the membranes, working over a bowl to catch the juice. Whisk the mint, vinegar, olive oil and honey into the juice and season to taste.

Heat a frying pan until hot, add the pine nuts and dry-fry for 1–2 minutes, stirring occasionally, until golden.

Meanwhile, heat a griddle pan until hot. Griddle the cheese slices for 1–2 minutes on each side until golden.

Divide the leaves and orange segments between 2 serving bowls, arrange the cheese on top and sprinkle with the pine nuts. Spoon over the dressing and serve immediately.

For haloumi with lemon & caper dressing, place 2 tablespoons olive oil in a bowl with the finely grated rind and juice of 1 small lemon, 1 tablespoon white wine vinegar, 1 teaspoon Dijon mustard, 2 tablespoons chopped parsley and 1 tablespoon capers. Season to taste and whisk together. Cut 250 g (8 oz) haloumi cheese into 8 slices and heat a griddle pan until hot. Cook the cheese for 1–2 minutes on each side until golden. Divide the cheese between 2 plates, drizzle with the dressing and serve immediately with warmed pitta breads.

prawn & rice paper wraps

Serves **2**
Preparation time **10 minutes**

3 **dried rice paper wrappers**
(banh trang), 20 cm
(8 inches) in diameter
½ **small carrot**, cut into thin
strips
2 **Chinese leaves**, shredded
25 g (1 oz) **bean sprouts**
4 tablespoons **chopped fresh
coriander**
125 g (4 oz) **cooked peeled
tiger prawns**
1 tablespoon **Thai fish sauce**
6 **mint leaves**
sweet chilli dipping sauce,
to serve

Place one of the wrappers in a bowl of warm water until softened and opaque. Shake off the excess water and lay on a plate.

Place the carrot, Chinese leaves, bean sprouts, coriander and prawns in a bowl and mix well.

Brush the middle of the wrapper with fish sauce, lay 2 mint leaves on it, then place one-third of the prawn mixture in a line down the middle. Fold in both sides of the wrapper, then roll up tightly.

Cover with a damp cloth and repeat with the remaining wrappers and filling. Cut each roll in half and serve immediately with the dipping sauce.

For prawn & lettuce cups, mix 200 g (7 oz) cooked peeled prawns with 125 g (4 oz) peeled and diced mango, 50 g (2 oz) bean sprouts and 2 tablespoons chopped fresh coriander. Arrange 8 outer leaves from Little Gem lettuces on a plate, rounded sides down. Fill the leaves with the prawn mixture and drizzle with a little sweet chilli dipping sauce. Serve immediately.

balsamic figs with parma ham

Serves **4**
Preparation time **5 minutes**
Cooking time **4–5 minutes**

8 **ripe figs**, halved
2 tablespoons **balsamic
vinegar**
extra virgin olive oil, for
drizzling
12 slices of **parma ham**
50 g (2 oz) **rocket**
salt and **pepper**

Arrange the fig halves, cut side up, on a baking sheet. Brush with the vinegar and lightly drizzle with oil. Season with a little salt and a generous grinding of pepper.

Cook under a preheated hot grill for 4–5 minutes until heated through and a little charred.

Arrange 3 slices of parma ham on each serving plate. Top with the grilled figs and scatter with rocket leaves. Drizzle over a little more oil and serve while the figs are still warm.

For minted melon with Parma ham, peel and slice a small, ripe melon and arrange on a platter with 12 slices of Parma ham. Scatter with 5 mint leaves, roughly torn, and drizzle with extra virgin olive oil.

croque monsieur

Serves **2**
Preparation time **4 minutes**
Cooking time **6 minutes**

4 slices of **crusty white bread**
1 tablespoon **Dijon mustard**
2 thick slices of **ham**
4 slices of **Gruyère cheese**
1 large **egg**
25 ml (1 fl oz) **milk**
1 tablespoon **sunflower oil**
salt and **pepper**

Spread 2 slices of the bread with the mustard, then top each with a slice of ham and 2 slices of cheese. Place the remaining bread on top to make 2 sandwiches.

Beat the egg and milk together in a shallow dish and then season to taste. Heat the oil in a large nonstick frying pan.

Place the sandwiches in the egg mixture, leave for 1 minute, then turn over and leave for another minute.

Cook the sandwiches in the frying pan for 3 minutes on each side until golden brown and the cheese has melted. Serve immediately.

For caramelized onion & cheese toasts, place 2 thick slices of white bread under a preheated hot grill and toast lightly on both sides. Spread each slice with 1 tablespoon caramelized onion chutney, and divide 125 g (4 oz) grated Gruyère cheese between them. Return to the grill and cook for 2–3 minutes until the cheese is bubbling and golden. Serve immediately with a crisp green salad.

chicken caesar salad

Serves **4**
Preparation time **7–8 minutes**

2 **Romaine lettuces**
1 **ripe avocado**, peeled,
   stoned and chopped
375 g (12 oz) **ready-cooked
   chargrilled chicken slices**
50 g (2 oz) **ready-made
   baked croûtons**

Dressing
6 tablespoons **low-fat crème
   fraîche**
2 **anchovy fillets in oil**,
   drained
4 tablespoons grated
   Parmesan cheese, plus
   extra to serve
finely grated rind and juice of
   ½ **lemon**
freshly ground black pepper

Place the crème fraîche in a food processor with the
anchovy fillets, Parmesan and lemon rind and juice.
Blend to make a smooth dressing and season to taste
with pepper.

Tear the lettuce into bite-sized pieces and place in a
bowl with the avocado. Pour over the dressing, toss
together and divide between 4 bowls.

Arrange the chicken on top and scatter with the
croûtons. Season with pepper and sprinkle with a little
Parmesan. Serve immediately.

For warm salmon Caesar salad, cut 4 skinless
salmon fillets, about 150 g (5 oz) each, lengthways
into 4 strips. Lightly oil a griddle pan and heat over a
medium heat. Cook the salmon strips for 1–2 minutes
on each side, until just cooked. Meanwhile, prepare
the dressing and salad as above, omitting the chicken.
Divide the salad between 4 bowls and top with the
salmon. Season with pepper and sprinkle with a little
grated Parmesan.

crab cocktail with baby avocados

Serves **4**
Preparation time **10 minutes**

4 tablespoons **mayonnaise**
2 tablespoons **Greek yogurt**
3 tablespoons **lime juice**
½–1 teaspoon **wasabi paste**
2 tablespoons **chopped fresh
    coriander**
200 g (7 oz) **fresh white crab
    meat**
4 ripe **baby avocados**
salt and **pepper**
ready-prepared watercress,
    to garnish

Mix together the mayonnaise and yogurt, then stir in
1 tablespoon of the lime juice and the wasabi paste, to
taste. Add the coriander and crab meat, season to taste
and toss to mix well.

Cut the avocados in half lengthways and remove the
stones, then brush with the remaining lime juice. Place
2 halves on each serving plate.

Fill the avocados with the crab mixture and garnish with
watercress. Serve immediately.

**For prawn cocktail with lime & coriander
mayonnaise**, separate the leaves from 3 Baby
Gem lettuces and divide between 4 glasses. Mix
6 tablespoons mayonnaise with 1 tablespoon lime
juice, 2 drops of Tabasco sauce and 2 tablespoons
chopped fresh coriander. Stir in 400 g (14 oz) cooked
peeled prawns, then spoon over the lettuce. Serve
immediately with lime wedges for squeezing.

butter bean & anchovy pâté

Serves **2–3**
Preparation time **8 minutes**

425 g (14 oz) **can butter beans**, drained and rinsed
50 g (2 oz) **can anchovy fillets in oil**, drained
2 **spring onions**, finely chopped
2 tablespoons **lemon juice**
1 tablespoon **olive oil**
4 tablespoons **chopped fresh coriander**
pepper
4–6 slices of **rye bread**, toasted, to serve

Place all the ingredients, except the coriander, in a food processor and blend until well mixed but still rough in texture. Alternatively, mash the beans with a fork, finely chop the anchovies and mix the ingredients together by hand.

Stir in the coriander and season well with pepper. Serve with toasted rye bread.

For butter bean & mushroom pâté, cook 250 g (8 oz) sliced mushrooms in 2 tablespoons olive oil with 1 finely chopped garlic clove until the mushrooms are tender and all the liquid has evaporated. Allow to cool, then follow the main recipe, using the mushrooms instead of the anchovies.

quails' eggs with serrano ham

Serves **2**
Preparation time **3 minutes**
Cooking time **6 minutes**

50 g (2 oz) **ready-made hollandaise sauce**
1 teaspoon **Dijon mustard**
2 slices of **serrano ham**
2 **English muffins**, split and toasted
25 g (1 oz) **butter**, softened
4 **quails' eggs**
watercress or **lambs' lettuce**, to serve

Mix the hollandaise sauce with the mustard and set aside. Heat a small frying pan until hot, add the ham and dry-fry for 2 minutes on each side until crispy. Meanwhile, spread the muffins with some of the butter and keep warm.

Brush a nonstick frying pan with the remaining butter and place over a moderate heat until hot. Break in the eggs and cook for 2 minutes.

Divide the muffin halves between 2 plates, arrange the eggs on top and spoon over the sauce. Serve immediately with the crisp ham and salad leaves.

For quails' eggs with asparagus, cook 250 g (8 oz) ready-trimmed asparagus spears in a large saucepan of lightly salted boiling water for 3–4 minutes, until just tender. Drain and keep warm. Meanwhile, place 4 quails' eggs in a small pan of cold water and bring to the boil, remove from the heat and leave to stand for 30 seconds. Peel and cut each egg in half. Prepare the mustard hollandaise as above. Divide the asparagus and eggs between 2 plates, spoon the hollandaise over the top and serve immediately with crusty bread.

greek feta & mint dip

Serves **4**
Preparation time **5 minutes**
Cooking time **2–4 minutes**

150 g (5 oz) **feta cheese**,
  crumbled
½ **small red onion**, thinly
  sliced
handful of **mint leaves**, finely
  chopped
200 ml (7 fl oz) **Greek yogurt**
8 wholemeal **pitta breads**
freshly ground black pepper
sliced black olives, to garnish

Mix the cheese with the onion, mint and yogurt, season with black pepper and stir gently to combine. Transfer to a serving bowl and scatter with a few sliced olives.

Cook the pitta breads under a preheated hot grill for 1–2 minutes each side until lightly toasted. Cut into strips and serve with the dip.

For Greek feta pittas, toast 4 pitta breads and slice open. Meanwhile, mix 12 halved cherry tomatoes with ½ small chopped cucumber, a small handful of sliced black olives and 200 g (7 oz) crumbled feta cheese. Whisk 2 tablespoons olive oil with 2 teaspoons red wine vinegar and a large pinch of dried oregano and season to taste. Pour over the salad ingredients and mix well. Place some shredded lettuce in each pitta bread and spoon in the Greek salad mixture. Serve immediately.

haloumi with paprika oil

Serves **4**
Preparation time **5 minutes**
Cooking time **5 minutes**

6 tablespoons **extra virgin
   olive oil**
4 tablespoons **lemon juice**
½ teaspoon **smoked paprika**
250 g (8 oz) **haloumi cheese**,
   cut into chunks
salt and **pepper**

Combine the oil, lemon juice and paprika in a small
bowl and season the mixture with salt and pepper.

Heat a heavy-based frying pan until hot, then add the
haloumi and toss over a medium heat until golden and
starting to soften. Transfer immediately to a plate, drizzle
over the paprika oil and serve with cocktail sticks to
spike the haloumi.

lentil & goats' cheese salad

Serves **4**
Preparation time **10 minutes**

125 g (4 oz) **baby spinach**
400 g (13 oz) can **Puy lentils
in water**, drained and rinsed
125 g (4 oz) **roasted red
peppers in brine** or **oil**,
drained and chopped
50 g (2 oz) **walnut pieces**
125 g (4 oz) **fresh goats'
cheese**, roughly crumbled

Dressing
2 tablespoons **balsamic
vinegar**
3 tablespoons **walnut oil**
1 teaspoon **Dijon mustard**
salt and **pepper**

Place the spinach, lentils, peppers and walnut pieces in a bowl and mix gently.

Whisk together the dressing ingredients in a small bowl and season to taste. Pour over the lentil mixture and toss lightly to combine. Divide between 4 bowls and top with the cheese.

For beetroot & goats' cheese salad, cut 8 ready-cooked beetroot into wedges and place in a bowl with 50 g (2 oz) toasted pine nuts and 150 g (5 oz) mixed salad and herb leaves. Whisk 1 tablespoon balsamic vinegar with 2 tablespoons olive oil and 2 teaspoons clear honey and season to taste. Pour over the salad and gently toss together. Divide between 4 plates and top with 200 g (7 oz) crumbled goats' cheese. Serve immediately.

naan bread pizzas

Serves **4**
Preparation time **2 minutes**
Cooking time **6–8 minutes**

2 **plain naan breads**, about
150 g (5 oz) each
4 tablespoons **mango
chutney**
125 g (4 oz) **ready-cooked
tandoori chicken** or **chicken
tikka**, chopped
½ **small red pepper**, cored,
deseeded and sliced
125 g (4 oz) **mozzarella
cheese**, grated
2 tablespoons **chopped fresh
coriander**
ready-made raita, to serve

Preheat the oven to 200°C (400°F), Gas Mark 6. Place
the naan breads on a large baking sheet and spread
with the mango chutney.

Arrange the chopped chicken and peppers on top and
sprinkle with the cheese. Bake in the preheated oven
for 6–8 minutes, until bubbling and golden.

Sprinkle with the coriander, cut in half and serve
immediately with raita.

For ciabatta pizzas, split a ciabatta loaf in half
lengthways. Cook under a preheated hot grill for
2 minutes on each side. Spread each cut side with
3 tablespoons sun-dried tomato paste, and then divide
125 g (4 oz) sliced mozzarella and 7 halved cherry
tomatoes between the pizzas. Cook under a preheated
hot grill for 3–4 minutes, until the cheese has melted.
Cut the pizzas in half and serve immediately sprinkled
with basil leaves.

tomato, hot pepper & tofu salad

Serves **2**
Preparation time **8 minutes**
Cooking time **1–2 minutes**

25 g (1 oz) **pine nuts**
1 **large beefsteak tomato**,
  thinly sliced
125 g (4 oz) **tofu**
50 g (2 oz) **hot piquante**
  peppers in brine or **oil**,
  drained and thinly sliced
3 tablespoons **snipped chives**
2 tablespoons **chopped flat**
  leaf parsley
40 g (1½ oz) **sultanas**
4 tablespoons **olive oil**
2 tablespoons **lemon juice**
2 teaspoons **caster sugar**
salt and **pepper**
crusty bread, to serve

Heat a frying pan until hot, add the pine nuts and dry-fry for 1–2 minutes, stirring occasionally, until golden.

Arrange the tomato slices on 2 serving plates and season lightly. Crumble the tofu into a mixing bowl, add the peppers, chives, parsley, pine nuts and sultanas and mix together.

Whisk the olive oil with the lemon juice and sugar, season to taste and toss with the tofu mixture. Spoon over the tomatoes and serve with crusty bread.

For spinach & tofu salad, crumble the tofu into a mixing bowl, add the herbs, pine nuts, sultanas and 3 tablespoons lime juice. Heat 2 teaspoons groundnut oil in a large frying pan. Add 1 crushed garlic clove, cook for a few seconds, then add 250 g (8 oz) baby spinach. Cook until wilted, then toss with the tofu salad and serve with crusty bread.

thai chilli chicken strips

Serves **4**
Preparation time **5 minutes**
Cooking time **5 minutes**

oil, for brushing
350 g (11½ oz) **chicken mini breast fillets**
lime wedges, to serve

Sauce
2 teaspoons **palm sugar** or **soft brown sugar**
1 tablespoon **ready-chopped ginger**
1 teaspoon **lemon grass paste**
3 tablespoons **sweet chilli sauce**
2 tablespoons **rice wine vinegar**
finely grated rind and juice of **1 lime**
4 tablespoons **dark soy sauce**

Brush a griddle pan with a little oil and heat over a high heat until hot. Meanwhile, cut each chicken fillet in half lengthways. Mix together all the sauce ingredients in a bowl, add the strips of chicken and mix well.

Cook the chicken strips in the hot pan for 3 minutes, brushing with any remaining sauce. Turn over and cook for a further 2 minutes. Serve immediately with lime wedges.

For Thai chicken soup, heat 1 tablespoon oil in a medium saucepan and add 2 tablespoons Thai red or green curry paste. Cook for 1 minute, then stir in 1 teaspoon lemon grass paste, 2 x 400 ml (13 fl oz) cans reduced-fat coconut milk and 1 tablespoon Thai fish sauce. Bring to the boil, reduce the heat, stir in 125 g (4 oz) drained canned bamboo shoots and simmer for 2–3 minutes. Meanwhile, roughly shred 350 g (11½ oz) ready-cooked chicken breast and stir into the soup with 2 tablespoons chopped fresh coriander. Simmer for 2 minutes until the chicken is heated through. Add 3 tablespoons lime juice and serve immediately.

salt & pepper squid

Serves **2**
Preparation time **2 minutes**
Cooking time **6 minutes**

150 ml (¼ pint) **sunflower oil**
4 tablespoons **cornflour**
½ teaspoon **salt**
1 teaspoon **freshly ground black pepper**
½ teaspoon **Chinese five spice powder**
250 g (8 oz) **raw squid rings**
lemon wedges, to serve

Heat the oil in a deep fat fryer or deep, heavy-based saucepan to 180°C (350°F), or until a cube of bread browns in 15 seconds.

Place the cornflour, salt, pepper and five spice in a large bowl and mix together. Add the squid and toss in the mixture to coat the rings evenly. Shake off any excess.

Cook half the squid in the hot oil for 2 minutes, then turn and cook for a further minute, until lightly golden. Remove with a slotted spoon and drain on kitchen paper. Repeat with the remaining squid. Serve immediately with lemon wedges.

For pan-fried squid with garlic, parsley & breadcrumbs, heat 1 tablespoon olive oil in a frying pan and add 1 teaspoon ready-chopped garlic. Cook for 1–2 minutes, until lightly golden. Stir in 250 g (8 oz) raw squid rings and stir to coat in the oil. Add 25 g (1 oz) fresh white breadcrumbs and cook, stirring from time to time, for 3–4 minutes until the crumbs are crisp and squid just cooked. Stir in 1 tablespoon chopped parsley and season to taste. Remove the pan from the heat and squeeze over 2 tablespoons lemon juice. Stir well and serve immediately.

chilled avocado soup

Serves **4**
Preparation time **10 minutes**

3 **ripe avocados**, peeled,
  stoned and diced
1 **small red onion**, roughly
  chopped
3–4 drops **Tabasco sauce**
3 tablespoons **lime juice**
600 ml (1 pint) **buttermilk**
4 tablespoons **chopped fresh
  coriander**
12 **ice cubes**
soft flour tortillas, warmed
  and cut into strips, to serve

Place the avocado in a food processor, reserving a handful for garnish, with all the remaining ingredients except the ice cubes and blend until smooth.

Divide between 4 glass bowls and top each portion with 3 ice cubes and some of the reserved avocado. Serve immediately with warmed tortilla strips

For avocado & bacon salad, cook 8 smoked back bacon rashers under a preheated hot grill for 3–4 minutes on each side until crispy, then drain on kitchen paper. Meanwhile, mix 4 tablespoons mayonnaise with 1 teaspoon wholegrain mustard and 2 tablespoons white wine vinegar. Peel, stone and slice 2 ripe avocados and place in a salad bowl with 375 g (12 oz) baby spinach and 12 halved cherry tomatoes. Cut the bacon into pieces and add to the salad with the dressing. Toss gently together and serve immediately with crusty bread.

smoked trout & horseradish pâté

Serves **4**
Preparation time **8 minutes**

200 g (7 oz) **hot-smoked
   trout fillets**
1 teaspoon **paprika**
2 tablespoons **lemon juice**
2 tablespoons **hot
   horseradish sauce**
100 g (3½ oz) **cream cheese**
salt and **pepper**
1 tablespoon **snipped chives**,
   to garnish
wholemeal toast or **crackers**,
   to serve

Flake the fish, removing any small bones. Place in a food processor with all the remaining ingredients and blend to a coarse pâté, scraping down the sides of the bowl from time to time.

Season to taste, garnish with the chives and serve with wholemeal toast or crackers.

For smoked trout scrambled eggs, beat 6 eggs with 2 tablespoons milk and season to taste. Melt 15 g (½ oz) butter in a nonstick saucepan over a low heat and add the eggs. Cook gently for 5–6 minutes, stirring occasionally, until the eggs are soft and creamy. Remove from the heat and stir in 200 g (7 oz) flaked smoked trout and 1 tablespoon snipped chives. Serve immediately with wholemeal toast.

poached eggs with spinach

Serves **4**
Preparation time **2 minutes**
Cooking time **8 minutes**

4 **vines of cherry tomatoes**,
   about 6 tomatoes on each
2 tablespoons **balsamic syrup**
   or **glaze**
1 **small bunch of basil**, leaves
   removed
1 tablespoon **vinegar**
4 large **eggs**
100 g (3½ oz) **baby spinach**
salt and **pepper**
4 thick slices of **wholemeal
   toast**, to serve

Preheat the oven to 200°C (400°F), Gas Mark 6, and bring a large saucepan of water to a gentle simmer. Place the cherry tomato vines in an ovenproof dish, drizzle with the balsamic syrup or glaze, scatter with the basil leaves and season to taste. Cook in the preheated oven for 8 minutes, or until the tomatoes begin to collapse.

Meanwhile, add the vinegar to the pan of simmering water, carefully break 2 eggs into the water and cook for 3 minutes. Remove with a slotted spoon and keep warm. Repeat with the remaining eggs.

Divide the spinach between 4 serving plates and place a poached egg on top of each. Arrange the tomatoes on the plates and drizzle the juices on top. Serve immediately with wholemeal toast.

For boiled egg, spinach & cress salad, boil 4 eggs in a saucepan of simmering water for 7–8 minutes. Meanwhile, divide 100 g (3½ oz) baby spinach and 24 halved cherry tomatoes between 4 serving plates. Cool the eggs under cold running water and peel and slice thickly. Place the sliced eggs on top of the salads, scatter with 20 g (¾ oz) cress and drizzle with a little olive oil and balsamic syrup. Serve with crusty bread.

moroccan-style hummus

Serves **4**
Preparation time **5 minutes**

400 g (13 oz) **can chickpeas**,
  drained and rinsed
1 tablespoon **tahini paste**
1 **garlic clove**, peeled
4 tablespoons **Greek yogurt**
1 tablespoon **rose harissa**
  paste, plus extra to drizzle
2 tablespoons **lemon juice**
salt and **pepper**
flat breads, to serve

Place all the ingredients in a food processor, reserving a few chickpeas for garnish, and blend to a smooth paste. If the consistency is too thick, add a little warm water.

Season to taste, transfer to a serving bowl and garnish with the reserved chickpeas and a drizzle of extra harissa. Serve with warmed flat breads.

For Moroccan pan-roasted chickpeas, drain a 400 g (13 oz) can chickpeas and dry on kitchen paper. Place in a bowl and sprinkle over 2 tablespoons Moroccan spice mix, such as ras el hanout, and stir well to coat. Heat 2 tablespoons olive oil in a large frying pan and cook the chickpeas for 5–6 minutes, stirring occasionally, until golden. Transfer to a bowl and serve hot or cold.

nachos with beans & cheese

Serves **4**
Preparation time **4 minutes**
Cooking time **3–4 minutes**

200 g (7 oz) **plain tortilla chips**
200 g (7 oz) **ready-made fresh tomato salsa**
400 g (13 oz) **can mixed beans**, drained and rinsed
200 g (7 oz) **jar sliced green jalapeños**, drained
125 g (4 oz) **mozzarella cheese**, grated

To serve
soured cream
ready-made guacamole

Place the tortilla chips in a shallow ovenproof dish. Spoon over the salsa, followed by the mixed beans, then scatter over the jalapeños and cheese.

Cook under a preheated hot grill for 3–4 minutes until the cheese has melted. Serve immediately with soured cream and guacamole.

For nachos with sweetcorn & chicken, arrange the tortillas in an ovenproof dish as above, spoon over the salsa and sprinkle with 6 chopped spring onions. Drain a 200 g (7 oz) can sweetcorn and scatter over the top with 2 shredded ready-cooked chicken breasts. Top with the grated cheese and cook as above until piping hot. Serve immediately.

chorizo, bean & tomato salad

Serves **4**
Preparation time **6 minutes**
Cooking time **3–4 minutes**

250 g (8 oz) **chorizo**, sliced
400 g (13 oz) **can butter
   beans**, drained and rinsed
250 g (8 oz) **cherry tomatoes**,
   halved
1 **small red onion**, thinly
   sliced
1 tablespoon **extra virgin
   olive oil**
1 tablespoon **sherry vinegar**
   or **red wine vinegar**
salt and **pepper**
small handful of c**hopped flat
   leaf parsley**, to garnish
crusty bread, to serve

Cook the chorizo in a large frying pan over a medium heat for 3–4 minutes, turning once, until crisp. Remove from the heat and stir in the butter beans, tomatoes and red onion.

Whisk the oil and vinegar together in a small bowl and season to taste. Transfer the chorizo mixture to a serving dish, pour over the dressing and toss well. Sprinkle with the parsley and serve immediately with crusty bread

For warm chorizo, chickpea & pepper salad, cook the chorizo as above, then stir in 400 g (13 oz) drained canned chickpeas. Remove from the heat and stir in 250 g (8 oz) chopped ready-roasted red peppers and 2 tablespoons chopped fresh coriander. Divide 200 g (7 oz) baby spinach between 4 bowls, top with the chickpea mixture and serve each portion with a spoonful of Greek yogurt.

french toast

Serves **4**
Preparation time **5 minutes**
Cooking time **4 minutes**

2 **eggs**, beaten
1 teaspoon **vanilla extract**
100 ml (3½ fl oz) **milk**
1 tablespoon **caster sugar**,
   plus extra for sprinkling
½ teaspoon **ground
   cinnamon**
4 thick slices of **bread**
25 g (1 oz) **butter**

Whisk the eggs with the vanilla extract, milk, sugar and cinnamon in a shallow dish. Place the slices of bread in the mixture, turning to coat both sides so that they absorb the liquid.

Heat the butter in a nonstick frying pan. Use a palette knife or fish slice to transfer the soaked bread to the hot pan and fry for 2 minutes on each side until golden.

Cut the toasts in half diagonally, sprinkle with a little caster sugar and serve immediately.

For apple & raspberry sauce, to serve as an accompaniment, heat 25 g (1 oz) butter in a frying pan, add 6 peeled, cored and sliced eating apples and fry for 2–3 minutes. Sprinkle over 1 tablespoon light soft brown sugar, ½ teaspoon ground cinnamon and 125 g (4 oz) raspberries and cook gently for 1–2 minutes. Pour over the French toast and sprinkle with extra caster sugar.

pasta, noodles & rice

spinach, ricotta & basil penne

Serves **4**
Preparation time **4 minutes**
Cooking time **6 minutes**

500 g (1 lb) **fresh penne**
1 tablespoon **olive oil**
1 teaspoon **ready-chopped garlic**
150 g (5 oz) **spinach**, finely chopped
2 tablespoons **chopped basil**
250 g (8 oz) **ricotta cheese**
100 ml (3½ fl oz) **dry white wine**
salt and **pepper**
Parmesan cheese shavings, to serve

Cook the pasta in a large saucepan of lightly salted boiling water for 3–4 minutes, or according to packet instructions, until al dente. Drain and return to the pan to keep warm.

Meanwhile, heat the oil in a large saucepan and cook the garlic for 2 minutes. Stir in the spinach and cook for 1–2 minutes, until wilted. Add the basil, ricotta and wine, season to taste and cook gently until the ricotta has melted.

Stir the drained pasta into the ricotta mixture, toss well and divide between 4 bowls. Serve topped with Parmesan shavings and freshly ground black pepper.

For pea, ricotta & mint tagiatelle, cook 500 g (1 lb) fresh tagliatelle in a large saucepan of lightly salted boiling water according to packet instructions, with 250 g (8 oz) frozen peas. Drain, reserving 2 tablespoons of the cooking water, and return to the pan. Stir in 250 g (8 oz) ricotta cheese with the reserved water until you have a creamy sauce. Add the finely grated rind of 1 lemon, 4 tablespoons chopped mint and 50 g (2 oz) freshly grated Parmesan cheese and stir well. Serve immediately with freshly ground black pepper.

gnocchi with sage & pine nuts

Serves **4**
Preparation time **5 minutes**
Cooking time **2–3 minutes**

500 g (1 lb) **fresh potato
  gnocchi**
50 g (2 oz) **unsalted butter**
12 **sage leaves**
25 g (1 oz) **pine nuts**
freshly ground black pepper

To serve
50 g (2 oz) **Parmesan
  cheese**, grated
crisp green salad

Cook the gnocchi in a large saucepan of lightly salted boiling water for 2–3 minutes, or according to packet instructions, until the gnocchi is plump and rises to the surface.

Meanwhile, heat the butter in a large frying pan over a moderate heat. When the butter starts to foam, stir in the sage leaves and pine nuts and cook for 1–2 minutes, until the sage is crispy and the pine nuts are golden. Add the gnocchi and toss to combine.

Divide between 4 bowls and serve sprinkled with the Parmesan and plenty of freshly ground black pepper. Serve with a crisp green salad.

For gnocchi with salami & spicy tomato sauce, cut 200 g (7 oz) salami slices into thin strips. Heat 1 tablespoon olive oil in a large frying pan, add 1 teaspoon chopped garlic and the salami and cook for 2–3 minutes. Stir in 350 g (11½ oz) ready-made tomato sauce with chilli. Bring to the boil and simmer for 3–4 minutes. Meanwhile, cook 500 g (1 lb) fresh gnocchi as above and drain well. Stir the gnocchi into the tomato sauce and serve immediately with freshly grated Parmesan cheese.

spicy thai crab noodles

Serves **2**
Preparation time **1 minute**
Cooking time **9 minutes**

1 tablespoon **groundnut** or **sunflower oil**
2 tablespoons **Thai red curry paste**
400 ml (13 fl oz) **can coconut milk**
2 teaspoons **Thai fish sauce**
1 teaspoon **lemon grass paste**
2 **fresh** or **dried kaffir lime leaves**
125 g (4 oz) **ready-trimmed green beans**
200 g (7 oz) **ready-cooked egg noodles**
125 g (4 oz) **cooked crab meat**
2 tablespoons **frozen ready-chopped coriander**
6 **holy basil leaves**

Heat the oil in a medium saucepan, add the curry paste and cook for 1 minute. Stir in the coconut milk and fish sauce.

Add the lemon grass paste, lime leaves and green beans, cover and simmer for about 6 minutes until the beans are tender.

Stir in the noodles, crab, coriander and holy basil. Cook for 2 minutes, until the noodles and crab are heated through. Divide between 2 bowls and serve immediately.

For spicy Thai prawn, ginger & spring onion stir-fry, heat 1 tablespoon oil in a wok or large frying pan and add 200 g (7 oz) raw peeled tiger prawns, 2 teaspoons ready-chopped ginger, 1 crushed garlic clove, 8 sliced spring onions and 1 deseeded and chopped small fresh red chilli. Stir-fry for 2–3 minutes until the prawns have turned pink. Add 3 tablespoons lime juice, 1 tablespoon Thai fish sauce and 1 tablespoon light soy sauce. Stir-fry for 1 minute, then stir in 2 tablespoons chopped fresh coriander. Serve immediately with ready-cooked noodles.

chinese fried rice

Serves **4**
Preparation time **3 minutes**
Cooking time **7 minutes**

2 **large eggs**
2 teaspoons **sesame oil**
2 tablespoons **sunflower oil**
500 g (1 lb) **ready-cooked rice**
125 g (4 oz) **frozen peas**
125 g (4 oz) **cooked peeled prawns**
125 g (4 oz) **smoked ham**, chopped
4 **spring onions**, finely chopped
2 tablespoons **light soy sauce**

Beat the eggs in a small bowl with the sesame oil. Heat the sunflower oil in a wok or large frying pan, add the rice and stir-fry for 2 minutes, then add the peas, prawns and ham and cook for a further 2–3 minutes.

Push the rice mixture to one side of the wok, then add the eggs. Allow to set for 10 seconds, then break up and stir into the rice. Add the spring onions and soy sauce and stir-fry for a further minute. Serve immediately.

For Chinese five spice rice with chicken & cashews, heat 1 tablespoon sunflower oil in a wok or large frying pan and add 350 g (11½ oz) stir-fry chicken strips. Stir-fry for 2–3 minutes until golden, then add 75 g (3 oz) unsalted cashew nuts and cook for 2 minutes. Add a bunch of chopped spring onions and 100 g (3½ oz) bean sprouts and stir-fry for 2 minutes, then stir in 500 g (1 lb) ready-cooked rice. Add 1 teaspoon Chinese five spice powder and cook for 2 minutes, then add 2 tablespoons soy sauce. Stir to heat through and serve immediately.

sicilian spaghetti

Serves **4**
Preparation time **4 minutes**
Cooking time **6 minutes**

500 g (1 lb) **fresh spaghetti**
2 x 50 g (2 oz) **cans anchovy fillets in olive oil**
2 teaspoons **ready-chopped garlic**
6 tablespoons **chopped flat leaf parsley**
¼ teaspoon **dried chilli flakes** (optional)
juice of 3 **lemons**
freshly ground black pepper
50 g (2 oz) **Parmesan cheese**, grated
rocket salad, to serve

Cook the pasta in a large saucepan of unsalted boiling water for 3–4 minutes, or according to packet instructions, until al dente. Drain and return to the pan to keep warm.

Meanwhile, drain the olive oil from the tins of anchovies into a large frying pan and add the garlic. Cook over a moderate heat for 1 minute, then add the anchovies. Cook for 2–3 minutes until the anchovies begin to soften and break up.

Add the parsley and chilli flakes, if using, then stir in the lemon juice. Add the drained pasta to the frying pan, season with pepper and toss to mix. Stir in most of the Parmesan, reserving a little for garnish. Divide the pasta between 4 bowls, sprinkle with the reserved Parmesan and serve immediately with a rocket salad.

For penne with anchovy, tomato & olives, cook 500 g (1 lb) fresh penne in a large saucepan of lightly salted boiling water according to packet instructions, drain and return to the pan to keep warm. Drain the oil from a 50 g (2 oz) can of anchovies into a frying pan with 2 teaspoons ready-chopped garlic. Cook for 1 minute, then add the anchovies and cook as above. Stir in 350 g (11½ oz) ready-made tomato sauce, simmer for 3–4 minutes to heat through, then stir in 50 g (2 oz) sliced black olives. Pour the sauce over the drained pasta, toss well and serve immediately with freshly grated Parmesan cheese and torn basil leaves.

spicy prawn jambalaya

Serves **4**
Preparation time **2 minutes**
Cooking time **8 minutes**

1 tablespoon **olive oil**
75 g (3 oz) **ready-diced chorizo**
1 **ready-chopped onion**
1 teaspoon **ready-chopped garlic**
½ **red pepper**, cored, deseeded and chopped
½ **green pepper**, cored, deseeded and chopped
1 teaspoon **hot chilli powder**
1 teaspoon **turmeric**
1 teaspoon **dried mixed herbs**
500 g (1 lb) **ready-cooked rice**
400 g (13 oz) can **chopped tomatoes**
150 ml (¼ pint) **chicken stock**, made with boiling water
350 g (11½ oz) **cooked peeled king prawns**
Tabasco sauce, to taste
salt and **pepper**
spring onions, chopped, to garnish

Heat the oil in a large saucepan, add the chorizo, onion, garlic and peppers and cook for 2 minutes, until the onion has softened and the chorizo has released its oil.

Add the spices and herbs, then stir in the rice and cook for 1 minute. Stir in the chopped tomatoes and chicken stock, bring to the boil and simmer for 4–5 minutes.

Stir in the prawns and heat through, then season to taste with salt, pepper and a few drops of Tabasco sauce. Divide between 4 bowls and serve immediately, garnished with chopped spring onions.

For chorizo & tomato rice, heat 1 tablespoon olive oil in a saucepan and add 175 g (6 oz) ready-diced chorizo, 1 ready-chopped onion, 1 sliced red pepper and 1 teaspoon ready-chopped garlic. Cook for 3–4 minutes until the oil has been released from the chorizo. Stir in 500 g (1 lb) ready-cooked rice and pour over 150 ml (¼ pint) dry white wine. Bring to the boil and simmer for 2 minutes. Stir in 400 g (13 oz) can chopped tomatoes with herbs and cook for a further 2–3 minutes. Season to taste, stir in 2 tablespoons chopped parsley and serve immediately.

vietnamese chicken noodle salad

Serves **4**
Preparation time **7 minutes**
Cooking time **3 minutes**

150 g (5 oz) **rice vermicelli**
½ **cucumber**, cut in half
  lengthways
250 g (8 oz) **ready-cooked
  chicken breast**, shredded
2 **carrots**, cut into thin strips
75 g (3 oz) **bean sprouts**
4 tablespoons **chopped mint**,
  plus extra to garnish
4 tablespoons **chopped fresh
  coriander**, plus extra to
  garnish
50 g (2 oz) **ready-roasted
  peanuts**, chopped

Dressing
2 tablespoons **rice wine
  vinegar**
3 tablespoons **sweet chilli
  sauce**
1 tablespoon **Thai fish sauce**
4 tablespoons **lime juice**

Place the vermicelli in a large bowl and pour over boiling water to cover. Leave to stand for 3 minutes, then refresh under cold water and leave to drain.

Meanwhile, remove the seeds from the cucumber using a teaspoon and thinly slice to form crescents. Place in a bowl with the chicken, carrots, bean sprouts, chopped herbs and peanuts, then added the drained noodles and toss well.

Whisk together all the dressing ingredients, then pour over the noodles and stir well. Serve garnished with extra coriander and mint leaves.

For crab & mango rice noodle salad, prepare the noodles as above, then toss in a bowl with 1 peeled, stoned and chopped mango, 2 x 175 g (6 oz) cans white crab meat, drained, 50 g (2 oz) rocket leaves and 4 tablespoons chopped fresh coriander. Whisk together 3 tablespoons lime juice, 1 tablespoon sunflower oil, ½ deseeded and chopped red chilli and ½ teaspoon caster sugar. Season to taste and pour over the noodles.

asian pesto with soba noodles

Serves **4**
Preparation time **4 minutes**
Cooking time **5–6 minutes**

350 g (11½ oz) **soba noodles**
2 **lemon grass stalks**
2 **small fresh red chillies**,
  deseeded and chopped
finely grated rind and juice of
  1 **lime**
50 g (2 oz) **fresh coriander
  leaves**
25 g (1 oz) **basil leaves**
2 teaspoons **ready-chopped
  ginger**
1 **garlic clove**, peeled
50 g (2 oz) **ready-roasted
  peanuts**
6 tablespoons **groundnut oil**
2 teaspoons **Thai fish sauce**
lime wedges, to serve

Cook the noodles in a large saucepan of lightly salted boiling water for 5–6 minutes, or according to packet instructions, until al dente. Drain and return to the pan to keep warm.

Meanwhile, remove the tough outer leaves from the lemon grass and roughly chop the core. Place in a food processor with all the remaining ingredients, except the oil and fish sauce, and blend to a smooth paste, scraping down the sides of the bowl with a spatula from time to time. With the processor still running, add the oil and fish sauce.

Stir the pesto into the warm noodles, divide between 4 bowls and serve immediately with lime wedges.

For rocket pesto, place 125 g (4 oz) rocket in a food processor with 50 g (2 oz) chopped toasted hazelnuts, 2 peeled garlic cloves and 50 g (2 oz) grated Parmesan cheese. Blend to a paste, then gradually add 6 tablespoons olive oil. Season to taste and serve with fresh pasta or gnocchi.

thai chicken & basil fried rice

Serves **4**
Preparation time **3 minutes**
Cooking time **7 minutes**

2 tablespoons **groundnut oil**
3 **garlic cloves**, chopped
3 **shallots**, thinly sliced
3 **small fresh red chillies**,
   finely chopped
2 **red peppers**, cored,
   deseeded and diced
250 g (8 oz) **minced chicken**
3 tablespoons **Thai fish sauce**
½ teaspoon **palm sugar** or
   soft brown sugar
2 tablespoons **light soy sauce**
500 g (1 lb) **ready-cooked
   rice**
large handful of **holy basil**

Heat the oil in a wok over a high heat until the oil starts to shimmer. Add the garlic, shallots, chillies and red peppers and stir-fry for 30 seconds, then add the chicken, fish sauce, sugar and soy sauce.

Stir-fry for 3–4 minutes, breaking the chicken up with the spatula, until the chicken is golden and cooked through.

Add the rice and basil and stir gently until piping hot. Serve immediately.

For pork & herb fried rice, chop 200 g (7 oz) lean pork into small cubes and use in place of the chicken. Cook as above, reducing the basil by half and adding a handful of coriander leaves and 6 torn mint leaves.

spicy chicken satay noodles

Serves **2**
Preparation time **4 minutes**
Cooking time **6 minutes**

1 tablespoon **sunflower oil**
1 teaspoon **ready-chopped ginger**
150 g (5 oz) **ready-cooked chicken**, diced
4 **spring onions**, thinly sliced
75 g (3 oz) **bean sprouts**
300 g (10 oz) **ready-cooked medium egg noodles**
fresh coriander, to garnish

Sauce
4 tablespoons **crunchy peanut butter**
2 tablespoons **sweet chilli sauce**
2 tablespoons **dark soy sauce**
2 tablespoons **lime juice**
100 ml (3½ fl oz) **water**

Whisk together all the ingredients for the sauce except the water in a small bowl.

Heat the oil in a wok or large frying pan, add the ginger and cook for 1 minute. Stir in the chicken, spring onions and bean sprouts and stir-fry for 2 minutes. Add the noodles and stir-fry for 1 minute.

Pour in the sauce and measurement water and stir to coat the noodles and chicken. Heat until piping hot, then serve immediately garnished with coriander leaves.

For spicy prawn noodle salad, mix 2 tablespoons peanut butter with 1 teaspoon sesame oil, 1 tablespoon chilli sauce and 2 tablespoons boiling water to make a dressing. Place 200 g (7 oz) cooked peeled prawns in a bowl with 300 g (10 oz) ready-cooked noodles, 2 sliced spring onions, 50 g (2 oz) halved mangetout and ½ sliced red pepper. Pour over the dressing and toss to mix. Serve garnished with a handful of chopped ready-roasted peanuts.

orzo risotto with pancetta & peas

Serves **4**
Preparation time **1 minute**
Cooking time **9 minutes**

900 ml (1½ pints) **chicken** or
  vegetable stock, made with
  boiling water
350 g (11½ oz) **orzo**
15 g (½ oz) **butter**
1 teaspoon **ready-chopped
  garlic**
150 g (5 oz) **ready-diced
  pancetta**
200 g (7 oz) **frozen peas**
handful of **parsley**, chopped
75 g (3 oz) **Parmesan
  cheese**, grated
salt and **pepper**

Place the stock in a medium nonstick pan, bring back to
the boil and add the pasta.

Meanwhile, melt the butter in a small frying pan and
add the garlic and pancetta. Fry for 2 minutes until the
pancetta is crispy.

Add the pancetta and garlic to the orzo with the peas
and continue to cook over a moderate heat for about
7 minutes until al dente, stirring from time to time to
prevent the pasta sticking and adding a little more water
if necessary.

Season to taste and stir in the parsley and most of
the Parmesan, reserving a little for garnish. Serve
immediately, sprinkled with the reserved Parmesan and
freshly ground black pepper.

**For orzo risotto with goats' cheese, pancetta &
sage**, cook the pasta in the boiling stock as above.
Meanwhile, cook 1 sliced red onion in the butter with
the garlic and pancetta until softened, then stir into the
orzo. When the pasta is al dente, stir in 125 g (4 oz) soft
goats' cheese, 2 tablespoons chopped sage and 50 g
(2 oz) freshly grated Parmesan cheese. Season and
serve immediately with freshly ground black pepper.

chicken & noodle miso soup

Serves **4**
Preparation time **2 minutes**
Cooking time **8 minutes**

900 ml (1 ½ pints) **chicken
    stock**, made with boiling
    water
2 x 18 g (¾ oz) **sachets
    miso soup paste** or
    2 tablespoons **miso paste**
2 teaspoons r**eady-chopped
    ginger**
4 **spring onions**, cut into thin
    strips
1 **carrot**, cut into thin strips
4 **baby pak choi**, halved
200 g (7 oz) **ready-cooked
    chicken breast**, sliced
300 g (10 oz) **ready-cooked
    medium egg noodles**

Place the chicken stock, miso paste and ginger in a
medium saucepan and bring back to the boil. Simmer
for 2 minutes.

Add the spring onions, carrot, pak choi and chicken and
simmer for 3–4 minutes more.

Stir in the noodles and cook for a further 2 minutes
to heat through. Divide between 4 bowls and serve
immediately.

For tofu & noodle miso soup, dissolve 1 ½ teaspoons
dashi (bonito flavoured granules) in 1.2 litres (2 pints)
boiling water or chicken stock in a medium saucepan
and add 2 x 18 g (¾ oz) sachets miso paste and
1 tablespoon wakame (dried seaweed). Bring to the
boil and add 200 g (7 oz) ready-cooked egg noodles
and 250 g (8 oz) diced tofu. Simmer for 2–3 minutes,
then stir in 2 tablespoons chopped spring onions. Divide
between 4 bowls and serve immediately.

ham & prawn fried rice

Serves **2–3**
Preparation time **3 minutes**
Cooking time **7 minutes**

4 **eggs**
1½ teaspoons **sesame oil**
2 teaspoons **light soy sauce**
1 tablespoon **groundnut oil**
125 g (4 oz) **raw peeled prawns**
125 g (4 oz) **ham**, shredded
1 tablespoon **ready-chopped ginger**
2 **garlic cloves**, crushed
5 **spring onions**, finely sliced
300 g (10 oz) **ready-cooked rice**
salt

Break the eggs into a bowl with 1 teaspoon of the sesame oil, the soy sauce and a pinch of salt and whisk lightly to combine.

Heat half the groundnut oil in a wok or large frying pan over a high heat until the oil starts to shimmer. Pour in the egg mixture and use a spatula to scramble it for 30–60 seconds, until just cooked, then remove from the pan and set aside.

Return the pan to the hob and heat the remaining oil. Add the prawns, ham, ginger and garlic and stir-fry for 1 minute until the prawns turn pink. Add the spring onions, rice, eggs and the remaining sesame oil and stir-fry for about 3 minutes until piping hot. Season to taste and serve immediately.

For chicken fried rice, omit the prawns and ham. Cook the eggs as above and remove from the wok, then heal 1 tablespoon groundnut oil and stir-fry the ginger, garlic and 250 g (8 oz) finely chopped chicken breast for 2–3 minutes. Add 2 tablespoons oyster sauce and cook for 1 minute, then add the spring onions and rice and continue as above.

smoked haddock kedgeree

Serves **4**
Preparation time **3 minutes**
Cooking time **6–7 minutes**

450 g (14½ oz) **smoked haddock fillet**
1 tablespoon **sunflower oil**
15 g (½ oz) **butter**
4 teaspoons **mild curry powder**
500 g (1 lb) **ready-cooked rice**
2 tablespoons **lemon juice**
2 tablespoons **frozen ready-chopped parsley**
4 **eggs**

Place the fish in a saucepan and pour over boiling water to just cover. Cook over a moderate heat for 3 minutes.

Meanwhile, heat the oil and butter in a large nonstick frying pan with a lid and add the curry powder. Cook for 1 minute, then add the rice and stir-fry for 2 minutes.

Remove the fish from the pan and flake into large pieces, removing any skin and bones. Stir into the rice along with 3 tablespoons of the cooking liquid, the lemon juice and parsley.

Make 4 wells in the rice and break in the eggs, cover the pan with the lid and cook over a low heat for 2–3 minutes, until the egg whites are just set. Serve immediately.

For curried vegetable rice, heat 1 tablespoon oil in a wok or large frying pan, add 1 ready-chopped onion and cook for 2–3 minutes until softened. Stir in 2 tablespoons tikka curry paste, then add 350 g (11½ oz) frozen mixed vegetables. Cook for 2 minutes, then stir in 500 g (1 lb) ready-cooked rice. Add 150 ml (¼ pint) boiling vegetable stock, then cover and simmer for 4 minutes until the vegetables are tender. Stir in 3 tablespoons full-fat natural yogurt and 4 tablespoons chopped fresh coriander and season to taste. Serve immediately with mango chutney.

pasta with tomatoes & basil

Serves **4**

Preparation time **2 minutes**

Cooking time **8 minutes**

2 tablespoons **olive oil**

1 **onion**, finely chopped

1 teaspoon **ready-chopped garlic**

500 g (1 lb) **small cherry tomatoes**

1 teaspoon **sugar**

1 teaspoon **balsamic vinegar**

10 **basil leaves**, shredded

350 g (11½ oz) **angel hair spaghetti**

salt and **pepper**

To serve

freshly grated **Parmesan cheese**

rocket

Heat the oil in a large frying pan, add the onion and garlic and cook for 2–3 minutes until the onion has softened. Stir in the cherry tomatoes, sugar and vinegar and cook for 5 minutes, stirring occasionally, until the tomatoes have softened and start to collapse. Gently squash some of them with the back of a spoon and season to taste. Stir in the basil.

Meanwhile, cook the pasta in a saucepan of lightly salted boiling water according to packet instructions until al dente.

Drain the pasta and toss with the sauce. Serve immediately with the grated Parmesan and rocket.

For pasta with creamy tomatoes & courgettes, heat 1 tablespoon olive oil in a frying pan and cook 2 chopped courgettes and 1 teaspoon ready-chopped garlic for 2–3 minutes. Add 200 g (7 oz) mascarpone cheese and stir in until melted, then add 200 ml (7 fl oz) passatta with herbs. Season and simmer for 2–3 minutes. Meanwhile, cook 500 g (1 lb) fresh penne according to packet instructions until al dente. Drain well, then stir into the sauce. Serve immediately with freshly ground black pepper.

egg fried rice

Serves **2**
Preparation time **3 minutes**
Cooking time **3–4 minutes**

2 tablespoons **groundnut oil**
4 **eggs**
2 teaspoons **ready-chopped ginger**
1½ tablespoons **light soy sauce**
300 g (10 oz) **ready-cooked rice**
2 **spring onions**, finely sliced
¼ teaspoon **sesame oil**

Heat the groundnut oil in a wok or large frying pan over a high heat until the oil starts to shimmer. Meanwhile, beat the eggs with the ginger and half the soy sauce.

Pour the egg mixture into the pan and use a spatula to scramble it for 30–60 seconds, until just cooked. Add the rice, spring onions, sesame oil and remaining soy sauce and stir-fry for 1–2 minutes until piping hot. Serve immediately.

For fried rice with Chinese leaves & chilli, follow the recipe above, adding 1 sliced fresh red chilli and 125 g (4 oz) shredded Chinese leaves once the rice is hot, and stir-fry for a further 30 seconds. Serve immediately.

meaty treats

parmesan & basil chicken

Serves 2
Preparation time **4 minutes**
Cooking time **6 minutes**

2 **chicken escalopes**, about
   0.5 cm (¼ inch) thick
4 tablespoons **plain flour**
25 g (1 oz) **fresh white
   breadcrumbs**
25 g (1 oz) **Parmesan
   cheese**, grated
2 tablespoons chopped **basil**
1 **egg**, beaten
1 tablespoon **olive oil**
salt and **pepper**

To serve
crisp green salad
lemon wedges

Season the chicken, then dust both sides in the flour, shaking off any excess.

Mix the breadcrumbs, Parmesan and basil in a shallow dish. Place the beaten egg in another shallow dish.

Dip the escalopes in the beaten egg on both sides, then in the Parmesan breadcrumbs to form an even coating.

Meanwhile, heat the oil in a large frying pan. When hot, add the crumbed escalopes and cook for 3 minutes on each side until crispy, golden and cooked through. Serve immediately with a crisp green salad and lemon wedges.

For chicken escalopes with caper sauce, heat 1 tablespoon oil in a large frying pan. Season 2 chicken escalopes with freshly ground black pepper and cook for 3 minutes on each side until cooked through. Remove from the pan and keep warm. Add 100 ml (3½ fl oz) boiling chicken stock to the pan with 50 ml (2 fl oz) white wine and bubble rapidly for 1 minute. Remove from the heat and whisk in 1 tablespoon capers and 15 g (½ oz) butter. Season, pour the sauce over the escalopes and serve with ready-cooked rice.

pepper steak with marsala sauce

Serves **2**
Preparation time **1 minute**
Cooking time **6–9 minutes**

1 teaspoon **sunflower oil**
15 g (½ oz) **butter**
1 tablespoon **mixed peppercorns**, crushed
2 **sirloin** or **rump steaks**, about 1 cm (½ inch) thick
125 g (4 oz) **ready-sliced mushrooms**
2 tablespoons **marsala wine**
6 tablespoons **soured cream**
salt
mangetout, to serve

Heat the oil and butter in a large frying pan. Press the peppercorns on both sides of the steaks to form an even coating.

Place the mushrooms and steaks in the hot pan and cook the steaks for 2 minutes each side for rare or 3–4 minutes each side for medium to well done, stirring the mushrooms occasionally. Remove the steaks from the pan and keep warm.

Add the marsala to the pan and cook for 1 minute, then stir in the soured cream and cook over a low heat until the sauce thickens. Season with salt, pour the sauce over the steaks and serve with mangetout.

For steaks with blue cheese sauce, mix 50 g (2 oz) soft blue cheese, such as dolcelatte, with 1 tablespoon half-fat crème fraîche and 1 tablespoon chopped chives. Season the steaks on both sides with freshly ground black pepper and place on a baking sheet. Cook under a preheated hot grill for 3–4 minutes on one side, depending how you like your steak cooked, then turn over. Grill for a further 2–3 minutes, then spread the cheese mixture over the tops of the steaks. Grill for a further minute until the cheese has melted. Transfer to serving plates and pour over any cheesy juices from the baking sheet. Serve with mashed potatoes

pork with apple & cider sauce

Serves **2**
Preparation time **3 minutes**
Cooking time **7 minutes**

1 tablespoon **oil**
15 g (½ oz) **unsalted butter**
250 g (8 oz) **pork fillet**, cut
    into 1 cm (½ inch) thick
    slices
1 **eating apple**, cored and cut
    into wedges
150 ml (¼ pint) **cider** or **apple
    juice**
4 tablespoons **crème fraîche**
6 **sage leaves**, chopped
salt and **pepper**
ready-cooked rice, to serve

Heat the oil and butter in a large frying pan over a high heat. Add the pork fillets and brown for 1–2 minutes on each side.

Add the apple wedges with the cider or apple juice, bring to the boil and simmer, uncovered, for 5 minutes until the liquid has reduced and the pork is cooked through.

Stir in the crème fraîche and sage, season to taste, then simmer for 1 minute, until heated through. Serve with rice.

For Cantonese pork, thinly slice 250 g (8 oz) pork fillet. Mix 1 teaspoon ready-chopped garlic with 3 tablespoons hoisin sauce, 2 tablespoons dark soy sauce, 1 tablespoon sherry, 1 tablespoon honey and ½ teaspoon sesame oil. Heat 1 tablespoon oil in a wok over a high heat, add the pork and cook until golden. Stir in the sauce, simmer for 3 minutes, then stir in 1 bunch sliced spring onions and 100 g (3½ oz) cucumber matchsticks. Heat through and serve immediately with ready-cooked rice.

smoked chicken salad

Serves **4**
Preparation time **8 minutes**
Cooking time **1–2 minutes**

50 g (2 oz) **pumpkin seeds**
300 g (10 oz) **skinless
  smoked chicken breast**,
  shredded
2 **red onions**, finely sliced and
  rinsed in water
150 g (5 oz) **cherry tomatoes**,
  halved
75 g (3 oz) **mixed salad
  leaves**
crusty bread, to serve

Dressing
1 **avocado**, peeled, stoned
  and diced
2 tablespoons **lime juice**
1 tablespoon **Dijon mustard**
salt and **pepper**

Heat a small frying pan until hot, add the pumpkin seeds and dry-fry for 1–2 minutes, stirring occasionally, until golden.

Make the dressing by placing all the ingredients in a food processor and blending them until smooth. Season to taste.

Place the chicken, onions, tomatoes, pumpkin seeds and salad leaves in a salad bowl and toss together. Drizzle over the dressing and serve with crusty bread.

For smoked chicken, broccoli & pasta salad, cook 250 g (8 oz) fresh rigatoni in lightly salted boiling water according to packet instructions, adding 250 g (8 oz) broccoli, broken into tiny florets, for the final 3 minutes of cooking. Drain and refresh under cold running water, then drain again. Prepare the salad as above, adding the pasta and broccoli instead of the pumpkin seeds and salad leaves. Make the dressing as above. Arrange the salad leaves in 4 serving bowls, top with the pasta salad and drizzle with the dressing.

stir-fried lamb with ginger & garlic

Serves **4**
Preparation time **3 minutes**
Cooking time **6 minutes**

500 g (1 lb) **lamb stir-fry strips**
1 tablespoon **Chinese rice wine** or **dry sherry**
2 tablespoons **dark soy sauce**
1 teaspoon **sesame oil**
2 teaspoons **ready-chopped garlic**
2 teaspoons **ready-chopped ginger**
2 teaspoons **cornflour**
1 tablespoon **sunflower oil**
6 **spring onions**, sliced lengthways
ready-cooked noodles, to serve

Place the lamb in a bowl and stir in the rice wine, soy sauce, sesame oil, garlic, ginger and cornflour. Mix well.

Heat the oil in a wok or large frying pan over a high heat. When it is very hot, add the lamb and sauce and stir-fry for 2–3 minutes until browned.

Add the spring onions and stir-fry for a further 2–3 minutes, until the sauce coats the meat. Serve immediately with noodles.

For griddled lamb with herbs & garlic, mix 1 teaspoon ready-chopped garlic with 2 tablespoons olive oil, 2 tablespoons lemon juice and 1 teaspoon each of dried oregano and thyme. Add 4 lamb steaks and coat in the mixture. Heat a griddle pan over a high heat, add the lamb and cook for 3–4 minutes each side. Serve with a mixed salad.

thai chicken with lemon grass

Serves **4**
Preparation time **2 minutes**
Cooking time **7–8 minutes**

2 **lemon grass stalks**
400 ml (14 fl oz) **can coconut milk**
1 teaspoon **ready-chopped garlic**
2 teaspoons **ready-chopped ginger**
2 teaspoons **ready-chopped red chilli**
2 teaspoons **palm sugar** or **soft brown sugar**
6 **kaffir lime leaves**
2 teaspoons **Thai fish sauce**
500 g (1 lb) **chicken stir-fry strips**
2 tablespoons **lime juice**
handful of **fresh coriander** or **holy basil leaves**

Remove the tough outer leaves from the lemon grass and chop the core into 2.5 cm (1 inch) pieces. Place in a large saucepan with the coconut milk, garlic, ginger, chilli, sugar, lime leaves and fish sauce.

Bring to the boil and reduce the heat to a simmer. Add the chicken, partially cover with a lid and cook gently for 6–7 minutes.

Stir in the lime juice and herbs and serve immediately.

For Thai massaman chicken curry, cut 350 g (11½ oz) new potatoes into small pieces and cook in a saucepan of lightly salted boiling water for 4 minutes until tender. Meanwhile, heat 1 tablespoon oil in a saucepan and add 500 g (1 lb) chicken strips and 3 tablespoons massaman curry paste. Cook for 3–4 minutes until the chicken is browned. Add a 400 ml (14 fl oz) can coconut milk, 2 kaffir lime leaves and 1 teaspoon Thai fish sauce. Bring to the boil, stir in the potatoes, cover and simmer for 5 minutes. Serve garnished with a large handful of unsalted peanuts.

sweet & sour minced pork

Serves **4**
Preparation time **1 minute**
Cooking time **8–9 minutes**

1 tablespoon **sunflower oil**
500 g (1 lb) **lean minced
  pork**
1 **ready-chopped onion**
225 g (7½ oz) **can pineapple
  chunks in natural juice**
1 **red pepper**, cored,
  deseeded and chopped
ready-cooked noodles,
  to serve

Sauce
4 tablespoons **tomato
  ketchup**
1 tablespoon **ready-chopped
  ginger**
2 teaspoons **cornflour**
2 tablespoons **dark soy sauce**
2 tablespoons **malt vinegar** or
  rice wine vinegar
1 tablespoon **palm sugar** or
  soft brown sugar

Heat the oil in a wok or large frying pan over a high
heat. Add the pork and onion and stir-fry for about
4 minutes until the pork is cooked through.

Meanwhile, drain the pineapple, reserving the juice
from the can. Whisk the pineapple juice with all the
sauce ingredients and set aside.

Add the pepper and pineapple to the wok and stir-
fry for 2–3 minutes, then pour in the sauce. Cook,
stirring continuously, until the sauce thickens. Serve
immediately with noodles.

For spicy Bombay minced pork, cut 200 g (7 oz)
new potatoes into 1 cm (½ inch) dice and cook in
lightly salted boiling water for 4 minutes. Meanwhile,
heat 1 tablespoon oil in a large wok or frying pan over a
high heat and add 1 ready-chopped onion and 500 g
(1 lb) minced pork. Cook for 3–4 minutes, then add
3 tablespoons medium curry paste. Stir in the potatoes,
225 g (7½ oz) can chopped tomatoes, 200 g (7 oz)
frozen peas and 150 ml (¼ pint) boiling chicken stock.
Bring to the boil, reduce the heat, cover and simmer
for 4 minutes, stirring occasionally. Season to taste and
serve with naan breads.

thai red beef curry

Serves **4**
Preparation time **2 minutes**
Cooking time **8 minutes**

1 tablespoon **groundnut oil**
625 g (1¼ lb) **beef stir-fry strips**
2 tablespoons **Thai red curry paste**
400 ml (14 fl oz) **can coconut milk**
150 ml (¼ pint) **beef stock**
1 tablespoon **palm sugar** or **soft brown sugar**
1 tablespoon **ready-chopped ginger**
1 **lemon grass stalk**, bruised
100 g (3½ oz) **mangetout**, diagonally sliced
100 g (3½ oz) **bean sprouts**
1 tablespoon **Thai fish sauce**
1 tablespoon **lime juice**
small handful of **fresh coriander**

Heat the oil in a wok or large frying pan over a high heat. Add the beef and curry paste and stir-fry for about 2 minutes, until the beef is lightly golden.

Add the coconut milk, stock, sugar, ginger, lemon grass, mangetout, bean sprouts, fish sauce and lime juice. Bring to the boil, then reduce the heat and simmer for 2 minutes, until the mangetout are tender.

Remove the lemon grass from the curry and stir in the coriander.

For Thai red vegetable curry, omit the beef and replace with 1 diced aubergine, 12 baby sweetcorn and 25 g (1 oz) drained canned bamboo shoots. Fry the curry paste in the oil for 1 minute, then add the vegetables and other ingredients as above. Simmer for about 7 minutes, until the aubergine is tender.

duck & soya bean salad

Serves **4**
Preparation time **6 minutes**
Cooking time **3–4 minutes**

200 g (7 oz) **fresh** or **frozen soya beans**
500 g (1 lb) **ready-cooked Peking duck**, shredded
1 **cucumber**, finely sliced
5 **spring onions**, very finely sliced, plus extra to garnish
Sichuan pepper, to garnish

Dressing
2 tablespoons **hoisin sauce**
4 tablespoons **dark soy sauce**
3 tablespoons **lime juice**

Cook the soya beans in a saucepan of lightly salted boiling water for 3–4 minutes, or according to packet instructions. Drain, refresh under cold running water and drain again.

Toss the duck with the soya beans, cucumber and spring onions in a large salad bowl. Make the dressing by whisking together all the ingredients.

Drizzle the dressing over the duck salad and toss gently to combine. Garnish with spring onions and a sprinkling of Sichuan pepper and serve immediately.

For poached salmon & green bean salad, cook 300 g (10 oz) green beans in a saucepan of lightly salted boiling water for 3–4 minutes. Drain, refresh under cold running water and drain again. Meanwhile, cook 3 boneless, skinless salmon fillets, about 175 g (6 oz) each, in a saucepan of lightly salted boiling water for 3–4 minutes, until just cooked but still pink in the middle. Flake the salmon into a salad bowl with the green beans, ½ finely diced cucumber and 75 g (3 oz) rocket and toss gently. Whisk together 2 tablespoons sweet chilli sauce, 2 tablespoons soy sauce and 3 tablespoons lime juice, drizzle over the salad and serve immediately.

gammon steaks with pineapple

Serves **2**
Preparation time **1 minute**
Cooking time **9 minutes**

2 **gammon steaks**, about
   200 g (7 oz) each
2 **canned pineapple rings**
mixed salad, to serve

Topping
6 tablespoons **fresh white**
   breadcrumbs
50 g (2 oz) **mature Cheddar**
   cheese, grated
15 g (½ oz) **butter**, melted
2 tablespoons chopped **flat-**
   leaf parsley

Place the gammon steaks on a baking sheet, snip the rinds at intervals to prevent curling and cook under a preheated hot grill for 5 minutes on one side. Meanwhile, mix together all the topping ingredients in a small bowl.

Turn over the steaks and place a pineapple ring on top of each. Return to the grill and cook for 2 minutes, then top with the cheese mixture and cook for a further 2 minutes until the topping is golden. Serve with a mixed salad.

For maple & mustard gammon steaks with fried eggs, mix 2 tablespoons maple syrup with 2 tablespoons wholegrain mustard. Spread half the mixture over one side of 2 gammon steaks and cook under a preheated hot grill for 5 minutes. Turn the steaks over and spread with the remaining glaze. Cook for a further 4 minutes until glazed and sticky. Meanwhile, heat 1 tablespoon sunflower oil in a large frying pan until very hot, break 2 large eggs into the pan and cook for 2–3 minutes. Serve the eggs with the gammon and some crusty bread.

creamy paprika chicken

Serves **4**
Preparation time **1 minute**
Cooking time **9 minutes**

15 g (½ oz) **unsalted butter**
1 tablespoon **sunflower oil**
500 g (1 lb) **chicken stir-fry
strips**
1 **red pepper**, cored,
deseeded and sliced
2 tablespoons **sweet paprika**
100 ml (3½ fl oz) **medium dry
sherry**
2 teaspoons **tomato purée**
4 tablespoons **crème fraîche**
or **soured cream**
1 tablespoon **frozen ready-
chopped parsley**
salt and **pepper**
ready-cooked rice, to serve

Heat the butter and oil in a large frying pan and stir-fry
the chicken strips for 3 minutes over a high heat, until
lightly browned.

Add the sliced red pepper and paprika and cook for
2 minutes, then add the sherry and tomato purée, bring
to the boil and simmer for 2–3 minutes.

Stir in the crème fraîche and parsley, season to taste
and heat through. Serve with rice.

For creamy pesto chicken with lemon, cook 500 g
(1 lb) fresh penne in a saucepan of lightly salted boiling
water according to packet instructions. Meanwhile,
heat 1 tablespoon olive oil in a frying pan with a lid, add
500 g (1 lb) chicken strips and cook for 3 minutes until
lightly browned. Stir in the finely grated rind of 1 lemon,
the juice of 2 lemons and 2 tablespoons fresh pesto
sauce. Simmer for 1 minute, then stir in 3 tablespoons
crème fraîche. Cover and simmer for 3–4 minutes. Drain
the pasta, stir into the chicken mixture and season to
taste. Serve immediately.

veal with sage & parma ham

Serves **2**
Preparation time **3 minutes**
Cooking time **7 minutes**

6 **sage leaves**
2 **veal escalopes**, about
    125 g (4 oz) each
4 slices of **Parma ham**
1 tablespoon **olive oil**
125 ml (4 fl oz) **chicken stock**
juice of 2 **lemons**
salt and **pepper**
French beans, to serve

Place 3 sage leaves on top of each escalope, season with pepper then wrap each escalope in 2 slices of ham.

Heat the oil in a large frying pan and cook the escalopes over a high heat for 2 minutes on each side until the ham is crispy. Transfer them to a warmed serving plate.

Pour the stock into the pan and bring to the boil, stirring to incorporate all the juices from the veal. Reduce the stock by half, add the lemon juice and simmer for 1 minute. Season to taste, pour the sauce over the escalopes and serve with French beans.

For veal & mushroom stroganoff, cut the veal escalopes into thin strips. Heat 1 tablespoon oil in a frying pan and stir-fry the veal with 1 teaspoon ready-chopped garlic for 2 minutes. Add 125 g (4 oz) sliced mushrooms and cook for a further 3 minutes. Stir in 150 ml (¼ pint) soured cream and 1 teaspoon Dijon mustard. Simmer for 3–4 minutes, then stir in 2 tablespoons chopped parsley. Season to taste and serve immediately with rice.

sausages with yorkshire puddings

Serves **4**
Preparation time **2 minutes**
Cooking time **8 minutes**

1 tablespoon **sunflower oil**
24 **cocktail sausages**
250 g (8 oz) **new potatoes**,
  cut into 1.5 cm (¾ inch) dice
8 ready-made **fresh Yorkshire
  puddings**
2 tablespoons **crispy dried
  onions**
4 teaspoons **gravy granules**
300 ml (½ pint) **boiling water**
salt
frozen peas, to serve

Preheat the oven to 200°C (400°F), Gas Mark 6. Heat the oil in a large frying pan and cook the sausages for 7–8 minutes, turning occasionally, until cooked through.

Meanwhile, cook the potatoes in a saucepan of lightly salted boiling water for 5–6 minutes until tender. Reheat the Yorkshire puddings in the preheated oven for 3–4 minutes, or according to packet instructions.

Place the dried onions and gravy granules in a jug, add the boiling water and stir until dissolved. Add the potatoes and onion gravy to the sausages and stir to heat through.

Arrange the Yorkshire puddings on 4 serving plates and divide the sausage mixture between them. Serve immediately with peas.

For frankfurters with Boston beans, heat 1 tablespoon oil in a large saucepan, add 1 ready-chopped onion and cook for 2–3 minutes until softened. Meanwhile, cut 8 frankfurter sausages into 2.5 cm (1 inch) chunks. Add to the pan and cook for 2 minutes. Stir in a 400 g (13 oz) can baked beans in tomato sauce, a 225 g (7½ oz) can chopped tomatoes, 1 teaspoon English mustard and 1 tablespoon Worcestershire sauce. Bring to the boil, cover and simmer for 4–5 minutes. Serve with crusty bread.

spicy cajun popcorn chicken

Serves **2**
Preparation time **4 minutes**
Cooking time **6 minutes**

150 ml (¼ pint) **sunflower oil**
1 **egg white**
75 ml (3 fl oz) **buttermilk**
1 teaspoon **smoked paprika**
250 g (8 oz) **ready-diced chicken breast**
50 g (2 oz) **plain flour**
2 tablespoons **Cajun seasoning**
salt and **pepper**

Chive mayonnaise
6 tablespoons **mayonnaise**
2 tablespoons **snipped chives**

Heat the oil in a deep fat fryer or deep, heavy-based saucepan to 180°C (350°F), or until a cube of bread browns in 15 seconds.

Meanwhile, lightly beat the egg white in a shallow dish and stir in the buttermilk and paprika. Season to taste then add the chicken and stir to coat. Mix the flour with the Cajun seasoning in another bowl.

Dip the pieces of chicken in the seasoned flour, then deep-fry for 3–4 minutes until golden brown. Remove with a slotted spoon and drain on kitchen paper.

Mix the mayonnaise with the chives and serve with the crispy chicken.

For spicy chicken fajitas, heat 1 tablespoon oil in a large frying pan and stir-fry 250 g (8 oz) chicken strips for 3–4 minutes until browned. Add 1 sliced red pepper and ½ sliced onion and cook for 2–3 minutes. Stir in 15 g (½ oz) fajita seasoning and cook for 2 minutes, then add 2 tablespoons lime juice. Divide the mixture between 4 warmed soft flour tortillas and add a spoonful of soured cream and ready-made tomato salsa to each. Roll up and serve immediately.

pan-fried gnocchi & chorizo salad

Serves **4**
Preparation time **2 minutes**
Cooking time **8 minutes**

2 tablespoons **olive oil**
400 g (13 oz) **fresh potato gnocchi**
4 large **ripe tomatoes**, roughly chopped
small bunch of **basil leaves**, roughly shredded
125 g (4 oz) **mozzarella cheese**, torn into pieces
100 g (3½ oz) **ready-sliced chorizo**
1–2 tablespoons **balsamic vinegar**
salt and **pepper**

Heat the olive oil in a large nonstick frying pan and add the gnocchi. Pan-fry for about 8 minutes, moving frequently, until crisp and golden.

Meanwhile, toss the tomatoes with the basil leaves and torn mozzarella, season to taste and arrange on 4 serving plates.

Add the chorizo to the pan of gnocchi for the final 1–2 minutes of cooking, until slightly crisp and golden. Scatter the gnocchi and chorizo over the salads and drizzle with a little balsamic vinegar to serve.

For pan-fried gnocchi, pancetta & rocket salad, cook the gnocchi as above, adding 100 g (3½ oz) chopped pancetta to the pan for the final 2 minutes of cooking. Meanwhile, place 200 g (7 oz) drained and rinsed canned chickpeas in a bowl and add 2 chopped spring onions, 10 halved cherry tomatoes, 1½ tablespoons red wine vinegar, 4 tablespoons olive oil and 2 tablespoons frozen chopped parsley. Season to taste and toss well. Arrange 125 g (4 oz) rocket on a large serving plate, top with the chickpea mixture, then sprinkle the gnocchi and pancetta on top and serve immediately.

beef, chilli & orange stir-fry

Serves **2**
Preparation time **3 minutes**
Cooking time **7 minutes**

1 teaspoon **cornflour**
150 ml (¼ pint) **orange juice**
2 tablespoons **sweet chilli sauce**
1 tablespoon **sunflower oil**
300 g (10 oz) **beef stir-fry strips**
1 teaspoon **ready-chopped ginger**
1 bunch of **spring onions**, sliced
100 g (3½ oz) **mangetout**, halved

Place the cornflour in a jug and stir in 1 tablespoon of the orange juice. Add the remaining orange juice and sweet chilli sauce and stir to combine.

Heat the oil in a wok or large frying pan and when very hot, add the beef and ginger and stir-fry for 3–4 minutes until browned. Add the spring onions and mangetout and stir-fry for 1 minute.

Add the orange juice mixture and cook, stirring continuously, for 1–2 minutes until the mixture thickens and coats the beef. Serve immediately.

For beef teriyaki stir-fry, mix 1 teaspoon ready-chopped ginger in a large bowl with 1 teaspoon ready-chopped garlic, 3 tablespoons dark soy sauce, 3 tablespoons mirin or dry sherry and 2 teaspoons soft brown sugar. Stir in 300 g (10 oz) beef strips. Heat 1 tablespoon oil in a wok or large frying pan, use a slotted spoon to transfer the beef to the pan and stir-fry for 4–5 minutes until browned. Stir 1 teaspoon cornflour into the remaining sauce in the bowl and add to the pan. Cook until the sauce thickens and serve immediately.

chicken, apricot & almond salad

Serves **4**
Preparation time **10 minutes**

200 g (7 oz) **celery**, thinly
  sliced
75 g (3 oz) **blanched
  almonds**, roughly chopped
3 tablespoons chopped
  parsley
4 tablespoons **mayonnaise**
400 g (13 oz) **ready-cooked
  chicken breast**, shredded
12 **apricots**, halved and
  stoned
salt and **pepper**

Place the celery, half the almonds, the parsley and
mayonnaise in a large bowl, season to taste and toss
to combine.

Add the chicken and apricots, stir lightly and transfer
to a serving plate. Garnish with the remaining almonds
to serve.

For chicken, apricot & tomato pittas, dice 12 stoned
apricots and toss with 3 diced ripe tomatoes, the
400 g (13 oz) shredded ready-cooked chicken breast,
3 tablespoons chopped fresh coriander and a large
handful of rocket. Whisk 3 tablespoons red wine vinegar
with 3 tablespoons olive oil, 1 teaspoon brown sugar
and 1 teaspoon soy sauce and pour the dressing over
the salad. Mix well and serve in warmed pitta breads.

fish &
seafood

salmon & potato pies

Serves **2**
Preparation time **1 minute**
Cooking time **9 minutes**

250 ml (8 fl oz) **ready-made cheese sauce**
75 g (3 oz) **frozen peas**
200 g (7 oz) **can pink** or **red salmon**, drained
400 g (13 oz) **ready-made mashed potatoes**
25 g (1 oz) **mature Cheddar cheese**, grated
salt and **pepper**

Place the cheese sauce in a medium saucepan and heat gently, then stir in the peas and simmer for 3 minutes. Flake the salmon and remove any skin and bones.

Add the salmon to the pan, heat through and season to taste. Divide the salmon mixture between 2 small ovenproof dishes.

Meanwhile, heat the mashed potatoes in the microwave according to packet instructions. Spoon the hot potato over the top of the fish and sprinkle with the cheese.

Place the dishes on a baking sheet and cook under a preheated hot grill for 3–4 minutes until golden and bubbling. Serve immediately.

For tuna & potato fish cakes, drain a 185 g (6½ oz) can tuna chunks in spring water and mix with 250 g (8 oz) ready-cooked mashed potatoes and 2 tablespoons chopped parsley. Season to taste and shape the mixture into 4 fish cakes, using lightly floured hands. Heat 1 tablespoon oil in a frying pan and cook the fish cakes over a medium to high heat for 3 minutes on each side until golden. Serve immediately with lemon wedges and a crisp salad.

seared swordfish with chermoula

Serves **4**
Preparation time **5 minutes**
Cooking time **5 minutes**

4 **swordfish steaks**, about
   175 g (6 oz) each
oil, for brushing
couscous, to serve

Chermoula
25 g (1 oz) **fresh coriander**
25 g (1 oz) **flat-leaf parsley**
2 teaspoons **sweet paprika**
1 teaspoon **ground cumin**
½ teaspoon **dried chilli flakes**
4 tablespoons **lemon juice**
2 **garlic cloves**, peeled
4 tablespoons **sunflower oil**
salt and **pepper**

Make the chermoula by roughly tearing up the herbs and placing in a food processor with all the other ingredients. Season to taste and blend to a rough paste. Smear the chermoula over both sides of the swordfish steaks.

Brush a large griddle pan or heavy frying pan with oil and heat over a high heat. Add the swordfish and cook for 1½–2 minutes on each side, until just cooked through. Serve immediately with herbed couscous.

For seared swordfish with green salsa, place 1 peeled garlic clove in a food processor with 2 tablespoons capers, 2 anchovy fillets, 4 tablespoons chopped dill, 4 tablespoons chopped flat-leaf parsley, 3 tablespoons olive oil, 1 tablespoon lemon juice and 1 teaspoon wholegrain mustard and blend until smooth. Cook the swordfish as above, without the chermoula, then remove the pan from the heat and pour in the salsa. Serve immediately with a crusty baguette and a handful of rocket.

crab & grapefruit salad

Serves **4**
Preparation time **10 minutes**

400 g (13 oz) **white crab meat**
1 **pink grapefruit**, peeled and sliced
50 g (2 oz) **rocket**
3 **spring onions**, sliced
200 g (7 oz) **mangetout**, halved
salt and **pepper**
4 chapattis, toasted, to serve

Dressing
85 g (3¼ oz) **watercress**, tough stalks removed
1 tablespoon **Dijon mustard**
2 tablespoons **olive oil**

Arrange the crab meat, grapefruit, rocket, spring onions and mangetout on a serving plate and season to taste.

Make the dressing by placing the watercress, mustard and oil in a food processor. Season with salt and blend until smooth.

Drizzle the dressing over the salad and serve with the toasted chapattis.

For warm prawn & asparagus salad, cut 200 g (7 oz) peeled potatoes into 1.5 cm (¾ inch) dice and cook in a saucepan of lightly salted boiling water for 6–7 minutes, until tender, adding 100 g (3½ oz) fine asparagus spears for the final 3 minutes of cooking. Mix 400 g (13 oz) cooked peeled prawns in a salad bowl with the rocket, spring onions and mangetout. Make the dressing as above, and lightly toss into the salad with the drained potatoes and asparagus. Serve immediately.

spicy grilled sardines

Serves **2**
Preparation time **5 minutes**
Cooking time **3–5 minutes**

6 large prepared **fresh sardines**
1 teaspoon **ready-chopped garlic**
finely grated rind and juice of ½ **lemon**
1 teaspoon **ground cumin**
1 teaspoon **hot smoked paprika**
1 tablespoon **olive oil**
salt and **pepper**

To serve
ciabatta bread, toasted
crisp green salad
lemon wedges

Use a sharp knife to make 3 slashes on each side of the fish, cutting through the skin and flesh to the bone. Arrange the sardines on a baking sheet.

Mix together all the remaining ingredients, season to taste then rub all over the fish to coat thoroughly.

Cook the sardines under a preheated hot grill or on a barbecue, turning once, for 3–5 minutes or until cooked through. Serve with toasted ciabatta, a crisp green salad and lemon wedges.

For mackerel with warm potato & mustard salad, thinly slice 200 g (7 oz) new potatoes and cook in a saucepan of lightly salted boiling water with 150 g (5 oz) halved trimmed green beans for 4–5 minutes until tender. Meanwhile, season 4 mackerel fillets and heat 1 tablespoon olive oil in a large frying pan. When the oil is hot, cook the fish skin side down for 2–3 minutes, then turn over and cook for a further minute. Mix 1 tablespoon capers with 4 tablespoons ready-made honey and mustard salad dressing and pour over the drained potatoes and beans. Divide between 2 plates and serve the mackerel on top.

crispy coconut prawns

Serves **4**
Preparation time **6 minutes**
Cooking time **3–4 minutes**

25 g (1 oz) **dried natural breadcrumbs**
75 g (3 oz) **desiccated coconut**
4 tablespoons **cornflour**
1 large **egg white**
150 ml (¼ pint) **sunflower oil**
250 g (8 oz) **raw peeled king prawns**
salt and **pepper**

To serve
lime wedges
sweet chilli dipping sauce

Place the breadcrumbs and coconut in a food processor and pulse together briefly to break up the coconut a little. Tip into a shallow bowl.

Season the cornflour with salt and freshly ground black pepper and place on a plate. Lightly beat the egg white in a shallow bowl.

Heat the oil in a deep fat fryer or deep, heavy-based saucepan to 180°C (350°F), or until a cube of bread browns in 15 seconds.

Meanwhile, toss the prawns, a few at a time, in the cornflour and shake off the excess. Dip them in the egg white to cover, then roll in the coconut mixture to make an even coating. Spread out on a large plate or baking sheet.

Cook the prawns in the hot oil for 3–4 minutes, lightly shaking to separate them, until golden brown. Remove them with a slotted spoon and drain on kitchen paper. Serve with lime wedges and sweet chilli dipping sauce.

For crispy sesame prawn toasts, cut 4 slices of slightly stale white bread into 4 triangles each. Place 300 g (10 oz) raw peeled king prawns in a food processor with 1 teaspoon ready-chopped ginger, ½ teaspoon salt, 2 chopped spring onions, 1 tablespoon cornflour, 1 teaspoon sesame oil and 1 egg white. Blend to a paste, spread thickly on the bread, then sprinkle with sesame seeds. Heat the oil as above and cook the toasts, a few at a time, prawn-side-down for about 1 minute until golden. Turn over and cook for a further 1–2 minutes. Remove with a slotted spoon and drain on kitchen paper. Serve hot.

vegetable broth with sea bass

Serves **4**
Preparation time **4 minutes**
Cooking time **6–7 minutes**

750 ml (1 ¼ pints) good-
quality **chicken** or **vegetable
stock**
2 tablespoons **olive oil**
4 **sea bass fillets**, about
200 g (7 oz) each
1 **fennel bulb**, trimmed and
cut into 8 wedges
12 **fine asparagus spears**
150 g (5 oz) **frozen peas**,
thawed
150 g (5 oz) **podded broad
beans**
small handful of **mint leaves**,
torn
small handful of **basil leaves**,
torn
salt and **pepper**
crusty bread, to serve

Bring the stock to the boil in a large saucepan. Heat
the oil in a large heavy-based frying pan.

Season the sea bass fillets and cook, skin-side down,
in the frying pan for 3–4 minutes until the skin is crispy.
Turn over and cook for 1 minute on the other side.

Meanwhile, cook the fennel in the simmering stock for
3 minutes, or until it is just starting to become tender.
Add the asparagus, peas and broad beans to the pan
and cook for a further 1–2 minutes. Season to taste.

Divide the vegetable broth between 4 bowls and
sprinkle with the herbs. Top each portion with a sea
bass fillet and serve immediately.

For Thai broth with prawns, bring 750 ml (1 ¼ pints)
fish stock to the boil in a large saucepan with
1 tablespoon lemon grass paste, 2 tablespoons ready-
chopped ginger, ½ teaspoon dried chilli flakes and
2 kaffir lime leaves and simmer for 3 minutes. Season
to taste, add 500 g (1 lb) raw peeled tiger prawns and
poach gently for 2–3 minutes, then add 125 g (4 oz)
sugar snap peas and 150 g (5 oz) ready-cooked rice
noodles and cook for 1 minute more. Serve immediately.

smoked haddock rarebit

Serves **4**
Preparation time **2 minutes**
Cooking time **7–8 minutes**

4 **smoked haddock fillets,**
about 150 g (5 oz) each
300 ml (½ pint) **ready-made
cheese sauce**
1 teaspoon **English mustard**
2 **egg yolks**
2 teaspoons **Worcestershire
sauce**
2 tablespoons chopped **flat-
leaf parsley**
25 g (1 oz) **mature Cheddar
cheese**, grated

To serve
**ready-made mashed
potatoes**
frozen peas

Place the haddock in a single layer in a deep frying pan
with a lid and pour over enough boiling water to cover.
Bring to the boil, cover and simmer gently for 2 minutes,
until half cooked. Carefully transfer the fish fillets to a
shallow ovenproof dish and keep warm.

Meanwhile, place the cheese sauce in a small pan
and heat through. Remove from the heat and stir in the
mustard, egg yolks, Worcestershire sauce and parsley.

Top the fish with the mixture, sprinkle over the grated
cheese and cook under a preheated hot grill for 3-4
minutes until bubbling and golden. Serve at once with
mashed potatoes and peas.

For smoked haddock, spinach & butter bean salad,
place 500 g (1 lb) smoked haddock in a pan and pour
over boiling water to just cover. Cook for 4–5 minutes
until cooked through, drain and leave to cool slightly.
Meanwhile, drain a 400 g (13 oz) can butter beans and
place in a bowl with 125 g (4 oz) baby spinach, 3 sliced
spring onions and 4 cooked beetroot, cut into wedges.
Flake the fish, removing any skin and bones, and add
to the bowl. Whisk 1 teaspoon Dijon mustard with
1 teaspoon white wine vinegar, 3 tablespoons soured
cream, 3 tablespoons light olive oil and 1 tablespoon
chopped dill. Season to taste, pour over the salad and
gently toss together. Serve immediately.

grilled cod with tapenade

Serves **4**
Preparation time **2 minutes**
Cooking time **8 minutes**

4 **chunky cod fillets**, about
   175 g (6 oz) each
oil, for brushing
salt and **pepper**
tomato and red onion salad,
   to serve

Dressing
50 g (2 oz) **stoned black
   olives**
2 **anchovy fillets in oil**,
   drained
2 teaspoons **capers in brine**,
   drained and rinsed
1 **garlic clove**, peeled
1 teaspoon **thyme leaves**
4 tablespoons **light olive oil**
1 tablespoon **red wine
   vinegar**

Brush the cod fillets with a little oil and season to
taste. Cook under a preheated hot grill for 4 minutes
on each side until cooked through.

Meanwhile, place the olives, anchovies, capers, garlic
and thyme in a food processor and pulse until roughly
chopped. Stir in the oil and vinegar.

Transfer the fish to serving plates and spoon the
tapenade dressing on top. Serve immediately with
a tomato and red onion salad.

For baked cod with a herb & anchovy crust, preheat
the oven to 200°C (400°F), Gas Mark 6. Mix 50 g (2 oz)
wholemeal breadcrumbs with 2 tablespoons chopped
parsley, the grated rind of ½ lemon and a 50 g (2 oz)
can anchovy fillets in oil, drained and chopped. Place
4 cod fillets, skin side down, on a baking sheet and
spoon over the crumb topping. Cook in the preheated
oven for 7–8 minutes until the topping is golden and
the cod cooked through. Serve with a crisp salad.

peppercorn-crusted tuna steaks

Serves **4**
Preparation time **3 minutes**
Cooking time **6–7 minutes**

4 **tuna steaks**, about 150 g
   (5 oz) each
2 teaspoons **mixed**
   peppercorns, crushed
250 g (8 oz) **sugar snap peas**
1 teaspoon **sesame oil**
2 teaspoons **sesame seeds,**
   lightly toasted
ready-cooked rice noodles,
   to serve

Dressing
2 tablespoons **light soy sauce**
4 tablespoons **mirin**
1 teaspoon **sugar**
1 teaspoon **wasabi paste**

Season the tuna steaks all over with the crushed peppercorns. Heat a griddle pan over a medium-high heat and griddle the tuna steaks for 2 minutes on each side until golden on the outside but still pink in the middle. Remove from the pan and leave to rest.

Drizzle the sugar snap peas with the sesame oil and steam over a saucepan of gently simmering water for 2–3 minutes or until tender.

Place all the dressing ingredients in a screw-top jar and shake vigorously until well combined.

Divide the sugar snap peas between 4 serving plates, cut the tuna steaks in half diagonally and arrange on the peas. Drizzle with the dressing and sprinkle with the sesame seeds. Serve immediately with rice noodles.

mussels with cider & herb broth

Serves **4**
Preparation time **2 minutes**
Cooking time **8 minutes**

15 g (½ oz) **butter**
1 **ready-chopped onion**
1 teaspoon **ready-chopped garlic**
2 kg (4 lb) **ready-prepared mussels**
150 ml (¼ pint) **cider**
150 ml (¼ pint) **crème fraîche**
2 tablespoons chopped **tarragon**
2 tablespoons chopped **flat-leaf parsley**
crusty bread, to serve

Melt the butter in a large saucepan and cook the onion and garlic for 2–3 minutes. Meanwhile, discard any mussels that are open and do not close when tapped.

Add the cider and mussels to the pan and cover with a lid. Cook over a high heat for 3–4 minutes, shaking the pan from time to time, until all the mussels have opened.

Discard any mussels which have not opened, then stir in the crème fraîche and herbs and heat through. Serve immediately with crusty bread.

For rustic seafood soup, heat 1 tablespoon olive oil in a large saucepan and cook 1 ready-chopped onion and 1 teaspoon ready-chopped garlic for 2 minutes until softened. Stir in 150 ml (¼ pint) white wine, a 400 g (13 oz) can chopped tomatoes, 450 ml (¾ pint) boiling fish stock and a sprig of thyme. Boil for 4 minutes, then stir in 200 g (7 oz) ready-diced cod fillet, 200 g (7 oz) raw peeled tiger prawns and 250 g (8 oz) ready-prepared mussels. Simmer for 3–4 minutes until the prawns have turned pink and the mussels have opened. Discard any mussels that do not open, season to taste and serve immediately with crusty bread.

prawn, mango & avocado salad

Serves **4**
Preparation time **10 minutes**

1 large **mango**, about 475 g
  (15 oz), peeled and stoned
1 ripe **avocado**, peeled and
  stoned
2 large **Cos lettuces**
16 large **cooked peeled king
  prawns**

Dressing
juice of 2 **limes**
1 teaspoon **palm sugar** or
  soft brown sugar
2 tablespoons **vegetable oil**
½ **fresh red chilli**, deseeded
  and finely chopped

Cut the mango and avocado into 2 cm (¾ inch) pieces
and separate the lettuces into leaves. Arrange the
lettuce, mango, avocado and prawns on a serving plate.

Make the dressing by whisking all the ingredients
together. Drizzle the dressing over the salad, toss
carefully to mix and serve immediately.

For creamy Marie Rose sauce, a more luxurious
dressing for this salad, mix 3 tablespoons mayonnaise
with 2 tablespoons double cream, 2 teaspoons
tomato ketchup, 1½ teaspoons Worcestershire sauce,
2–3 drops Tabasco sauce, 1 tablespoon lemon juice
and 1 tablespoon brandy. Season to taste with salt and
pepper and drizzle over the salad.

japanese-style crispy fish goujons

Serves **2**
Preparation time **4 minutes**
Cooking time **6 minutes**

150 ml (¼ pint) **sunflower oil**
200 g (7 oz) **cod** or **haddock loins**
25 g (1 oz) **cornflour**
1 **egg**, beaten
100 g (3½ oz) **dried panko** (Japanese breadcrumbs)
salt and **pepper**
lemon wedges, to serve

Wasabi mayonnaise
50 g (2 oz) **mayonnaise**
½ teaspoon **wasabi paste**

Cut the fish into 1 cm (½ inch) strips and season to taste. Place the cornflour, egg and breadcrumbs in 3 separate shallow bowls, then dip the fish pieces first in the cornflour, then in the egg, and finally in the breadcrumbs to coat them and spread out on a large plate or baking sheet.

Meanwhile, heat the oil in a deep fat fryer or deep, heavy-based saucepan to 180°C (350°F), or until a cube of bread browns in 15 seconds.

Cook the fish in the hot oil for 3–4 minutes until golden brown, then remove with a slotted spoon and drain on kitchen paper. Mix the mayonnaise with the wasabi. Serve the crispy fish immediately with the spicy mayonnaise and some lemon wedges.

For fish goujon sandwiches, prepare and cook the fish as above. Meanwhile, split 2 large soft bread rolls and spread with a little softened butter. Place the fish goujons on the bottom halves and top each with 1–2 tablespoons ready-made tartare sauce and a handful of rocket leaves. Replace the tops of the rolls and serve immediately with lemon wedges.

spiced mackerel fillets

Serves **4**

Preparation time **4 minutes**

Cooking time **5–6 minutes**

2 tablespoons **olive oil**

1 tablespoon **smoked paprika**

1 teaspoon **cayenne pepper**

8 **mackerel fillets**

2 **limes**, quartered

salt and **pepper**

rocket salad, to serve

Mix the oil with the paprika and cayenne and season to taste. Make 3 shallow cuts in the skin of each mackerel fillet and brush all over with the spiced oil.

Cook the lime quarters with the mackerel fillets on a hot barbecue or under a preheated hot grill, skin side first, for 4–5 minutes until the skin is crispy and the limes are charred.

Turn the fish over and cook for a further minute on the other side. Serve with a rocket salad.

For black pepper & bay mackerel, mix together 4 very finely shredded bay leaves, 1 crushed garlic clove, ½ teaspoon freshly ground black pepper, a pinch of salt and 4 tablespoons olive oil. Rub the marinade over and into the cavities of 4 whole prepared mackerel. Cook on a hot barbecue or under a preheated hot grill for 3–4 minutes on each side. Serve with a tomato salad.

cod tacos with lime & coriander

Serves **4**
Preparation time **4 minutes**
Cooking time **6 minutes**

625 g (1¼ lb) **cod** or
   haddock loins, cut into
   2.5cm (1 inch) cubes
2 tablespoons **Cajun
   seasoning**
8 **taco shells**
1 tablespoon **groundnut oil**
2 tablespoons **lime juice**
1 small **Cos lettuce**, shredded
4 tablespoons chopped **fresh
   coriander**
200 g (7 oz) **ready-made
   guacamole**
200 g (7 oz) **ready-made
   fresh tomato salsa**

Preheat the oven to 180°C (350°F), Gas Mark 4.
Place the fish in a large bowl and sprinkle over the
Cajun seasoning. Gently shake the bowl to coat the fish
pieces in the seasoning.

Arrange the taco shells upright in an ovenproof dish
and warm in the preheated oven for 5 minutes.

Meanwhile, heat the oil in a large frying pan and cook
the fish pieces for 2–3 minutes on each side until
cooked through. Carefully transfer the fish to a bowl
and drizzle with the lime juice.

Fill the taco shells with the lettuce and top with the fish.
Scatter the coriander on top and serve immediately with
the tomato salsa and guacamole.

For Cajun cod tortillas with lime crème fraîche,
sprinkle 1 tablespoon Cajun seasoning over 4 cod
fillets, about 175 g (6 oz) each. Melt 25 g (1 oz) butter
in a frying pan and cook the fish for 3–4 minutes each
side, until cooked through. Meanwhile, mix 125 ml
(4 fl oz) crème fraîche with 1 tablespoon lime juice and
2 tablespoons chopped fresh coriander. Serve the fish
with warmed soft flour tortillas, the crème fraîche and a
crisp salad.

mixed seafood with peppercorns

Serves **4**
Preparation time **5 minutes**
Cooking time **5 minutes**

3 tablespoons **groundnut oil**
2 **garlic cloves**, finely chopped
4 **scallops**, quartered
6 **crab sticks**, halved
200 g (7 oz) **cooked peeled
   tiger prawns**
1 tablespoon **Thai fish sauce**
1 tablespoon **oyster sauce**
1 tablespoon **light soy sauce**
1 teaspoon **palm sugar** or
   soft brown sugar
2 tablespoons **fresh green
   peppercorns**
ready-cooked rice, to serve

Heat the oil in a wok or large frying pan over a high heat until the oil starts to shimmer. Add the garlic and stir-fry for a few seconds, then add the scallops and stir-fry for 1 minute until golden.

Add the crab sticks, prawns, fish sauce, oyster sauce, soy sauce, sugar and peppercorns, in that order, giving the dish a quick stir between each addition.

Cook for 1 more minute, until all the fish is heated through and well coated in the sauce. Serve with rice.

For coconut rice, to serve as an accompaniment, heat 1 tablespoon groundnut oil in a wok or large frying pan and add 5 tablespoons coconut milk. Bring to the boil with 1 teaspoon Thai fish sauce and stir in 250 g (8 oz) ready-cooked rice. Heat through, season to taste, add a squeeze of lime juice and serve with the seafood.

swordfish with sage pangritata

Serves **4**
Preparation time **2 minutes**
Cooking time **8 minutes**

250 g (8 oz) **fine green beans**
5 tablespoons **extra virgin
  olive oil**, plus extra for
  drizzling
1 tablespoon **ready-chopped
  garlic**
2 tablespoons chopped **sage
  leaves**
125 g (4 oz) **fresh white
  breadcrumbs**
finely grated rind and juice of
  1 **lemon**
4 **swordfish steaks**, about
  200 g (7 oz) each
salt and **pepper**

Cook the beans in a saucepan of lightly salted boiling water for 3 minutes until just tender.

Meanwhile, heat 4 tablespoons of the oil in a frying pan and cook the garlic, sage, breadcrumbs and lemon rind, stirring constantly, for 5 minutes until crisp and golden. Drain the pangritata thoroughly on kitchen paper.

Heat a griddle pan until hot. Brush the swordfish with the remaining oil, season to taste and sear in the griddle pan for 1½ minutes on each side.

Season the beans to taste and toss with a little of the lemon juice and a drizzle of oil.

Transfer the swordfish to 4 serving plates, drizzle with the remaining lemon juice and top with the pangritata. Serve with the beans.

For swordfish with bacon pangritata and creamy leeks, cook 250 g (8 oz) chopped leeks in a saucepan of lightly salted boiling water for 3 minutes. Make the pangritata as above, adding 3 finely chopped streaky bacon rashers, and drain on kitchen paper. Toss the drained leeks with 200 ml (7 fl oz) crème fraîche mixed with ½ teaspoon Dijon mustard and season to taste. Cook the swordfish as above and serve on a bed of creamy leeks, topped with the bacon pangritata.

vegetables

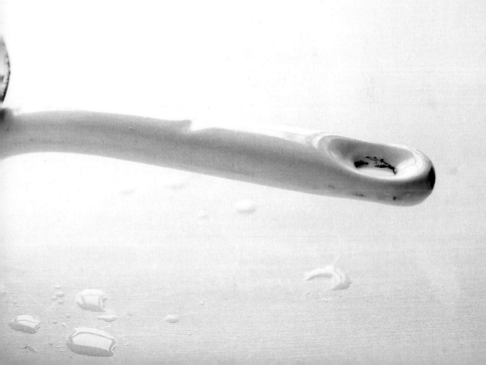

caramelized onion & brie tarts

Serves **4**
Preparation time **2 minutes**
Cooking time **7–8 minutes**

8 **ready-made savoury tart cases**, about 9 cm (3½ inches)
8 tablespoons **caramelized onion chutney**
125 g (4 oz) **Brie cheese**, cut into 8 slices
thyme sprigs, to garnish

Preheat the oven to 180°C (350°F), Gas Mark 4. Place the tart cases on a baking sheet and spread 1 tablespoon of chutney in the bottom of each. Top with the Brie.

Cook in the preheated oven for 7–8 minutes until the cheese melts. Garnish with thyme sprigs and serve hot.

For creamy roasted pepper tarts, beat 125 g (4 oz) light garlic and herb cream cheese with 1 egg and 25 g (1 oz) grated Parmesan cheese. Spoon the mixture into 8 savoury tart cases on a baking sheet. Top with 100 g (3½ oz) chopped ready-roasted red peppers and cook in a preheated oven at 190°C (375°F), Gas Mark 5, for 8 minutes. Serve with lambs' lettuce.

paneer, pea & spinach curry

Serves **4**
Preparation time **2 minutes**
Cooking time **8 minutes**

2 tablespoons **groundnut oil**
1 **ready-chopped onion**
1 teaspoon **ready-chopped garlic**
2 teaspoons **ready-chopped ginger**
250 g (8 oz) **paneer cheese**
2 tablespoons **medium curry powder**
400 ml (14 fl oz) **can coconut milk**
250 g (8 oz) **frozen peas**
225 g (7½ oz) **baby spinach**
salt and **pepper**
naan breads, to serve

Heat the oil in a large saucepan and cook the onion, garlic and ginger over a low hear for 2–3 minutes. Meanwhile, cut the paneer into 1.5 cm (¾ inch) cubes.

Add the curry powder and cook for 1 minute, then stir in the paneer. Stir-fry for a further minute.

Pour over the coconut milk and add the peas. Cover and simmer for 4 minutes, until the peas are tender. Stir in the spinach and cook for a further minute, until the spinach has wilted. Season to taste and serve immediately with naan breads.

For tandoori paneer & mushroom kebabs, mix 4 tablespoons natural yogurt with 2 tablespoons tandoori curry paste and 1 tablespoon lemon juice. Stir in the paneer cubes and 16 button mushrooms to coat. Thread on to 4 metal skewers and cook under a preheated hot grill or on a barbecue for 8 minutes, turning occasionally and brushing with any remaining yogurt mixture. Serve with salad and naan breads.

mushrooms with mascarpone

Serves **4**
Preparation time **2 minutes**
Cooking time **8 minutes**

25 g (1 oz) **butter**
1 teaspoon **ready-chopped garlic**
500 g (1 lb) **ready-sliced mushrooms**
2 tablespoons **marsala wine** or **sherry**
3 tablespoons **mascarpone cheese**
2 tablespoons roughly chopped **tarragon**
salt and **pepper**
crusty bread, to serve

Melt the butter in a large frying pan. When foaming, add the garlic and mushrooms and cook over a high heat for 5 minutes, stirring occasionally, until the mushrooms are lightly browned.

Stir in the marsala or sherry and simmer for 2 minutes. Add the mascarpone and stir until melted into the sauce, then stir in the tarragon. Season to taste and serve immediately with crusty bread.

For mushroom stroganoff, cook 500 g (1 lb) ready-sliced mushrooms in 25 g (1 oz) butter as above until lightly browned. Stir in 1 teaspoon paprika and 1 tablespoon brandy and cook for 1 minute. Add 300 ml (½ pint) soured cream, simmer for 2 minutes then season to taste and stir in 2 tablespoons chopped parsley. Serve immediately with ready-cooked rice.

mixed vegetable hash

Serves **2**
Preparation time **2 minutes**
Cooking time **8 minutes**

125 g (4 oz) **curly kale**, sliced
1 tablespoon **sunflower oil**
1 small **ready-chopped onion**
1 tablespoon **wholegrain mustard**
450 g (14½ oz) **ready-made mixed vegetable mash**, such as potato, carrot and swede
salt and **pepper**

Cook the kale in a large saucepan of lightly salted boiling water for 3 minutes. Meanwhile, heat the oil in a nonstick frying pan and cook the onion for 2 minutes until softened.

Stir the mustard into the vegetable mash and add to the pan. Add the drained kale, season to taste and mix well. Cook over a medium heat for 3 minutes on one side until golden, then flip the mixture over and cook for a further 2 minutes until piping hot. Serve immediately.

For minted pea & potato hash, cook 200 g (7 oz) frozen peas according to packet instructions, then drain and roughly mash with a potato masher. Stir 450 g (14½ oz) ready-mashed potatoes into the peas with 2 tablespoons freshly chopped mint and season to taste. Meanwhile, heat 1 tablespoon oil in a nonstick frying pan and add the potato and pea mixture. Cook for 3 minutes each side until golden. Serve immediately.

garlicky choi sum

Serves **4**
Preparation time **5 minutes**
Cooking time **5 minutes**

2 tablespoons **groundnut oil**
3 **garlic cloves**, sliced
1 teaspoon **salt**
500 g (1 lb) **choi sum**,
   trimmed and cut into 5 cm
   (2 inch) pieces
2 tablespoons **Chinese rice
   wine** or **dry sherry**
150 ml (¼ pint) **water**
1 teaspoon **sesame oil**

Heat the oil in a wok or large frying pan over a high heat until the oil starts to shimmer. Add the garlic and salt and stir-fry for 15 seconds, then add the choi sum and stir-fry for 1 minute.

Add the rice wine and measurement water and stir-fry for 2–3 minutes, until the choi sum is tender and most of the liquid has evaporated.

Stir in the sesame oil and serve immediately.

For pak choi with water chestnuts & garlic, follow the recipe above, replacing the choi sum with 500 g (1 lb) pak choi, cut into 5 cm (2 inch) lengths, and 4 sliced canned water chestnuts.

broccoli & cauliflower gratin

Serves **4**
Preparation time **2 minutes**
Cooking time **7–8 minutes**

500 g (1 lb) small **cauliflower florets**
250 g (8 oz) small **broccoli florets**
350 g (11½ oz) **ready-made 4-cheese sauce**
8 **sun-dried tomatoes,** drained and roughly chopped
50 g (2 oz) **mature Cheddar cheese**, grated
salt

Cook the cauliflower in a large saucepan of lightly salted boiling water for 2 minutes, then add the broccoli and cook for a further 3 minutes, until the vegetables are just tender. Drain well.

Meanwhile, place the sauce in a medium saucepan and cook over a moderate heat, stirring occasionally, until simmering. Stir in the sun-dried tomatoes, cauliflower and broccoli and mix together.

Transfer to a shallow ovenproof dish, sprinkle with the grated cheese and cook under a preheated hot grill for 2–3 minutes, until the cheese has melted.

For stir-fried broccoli with oyster sauce, cook 500 g (1 lb) tenderstem broccoli in a saucepan of lightly salted boiling water for 3–4 minutes. Plunge into cold water, then drain well. Meanwhile, blend 2 teaspoons cornflour with 2 tablespoons water in a small bowl. Heat 1 tablespoon sunflower oil in a wok or large frying pan and add 1 teaspoon ready-chopped garlic and the broccoli and stir-fry for 1 minute. Add 4 tablespoons oyster sauce, cook for 1 minute, then stir in the blended cornflour. When the sauce starts to thicken, stir in ½ teaspoon sesame oil. Serve with ready-cooked rice.

spinach, potato & ricotta frittata

Serves **4**
Preparation time **1 minute**
Cooking time **7–9 minutes**

200 g (7 oz) **new potatoes**,
  thinly sliced
1 tablespoon **olive oil**
100 g (3½ oz) **baby spinach**
6 **eggs**
2 tablespoons snipped **chives**
125 g (4 oz) **ricotta cheese**
salt and **pepper**

Cook the potatoes in a saucepan of lightly salted boiling water for 2–3 minutes until just tender. Meanwhile, heat the oil in a 28 cm (11 inch) ovenproof frying pan, add the spinach and cook for 1 minute until wilted.

Beat the eggs in a small bowl with the chives and season to taste. Drain the potatoes and stir into the pan with the spinach, then add the eggs and stir briefly. Cook without stirring over a medium heat for 3–4 minutes until almost set.

Dot the ricotta over the frittata and continue to cook under a preheated hot grill for 2 minutes until golden. Cut into wedges and serve immediately.

For sweetcorn & roasted pepper frittata, heat 1 tablespoon olive oil in a frying pan as above, then stir in 150 g (5 oz) chopped ready-roasted red peppers and 200 g (7 oz) canned sweetcorn and cook for 1 minute. Beat 6 eggs with 2 tablespoons chopped parsley and season to taste. Pour into the pan and cook as above, then sprinkle with 125 g (4 oz) grated Cheddar cheese and grill until golden.

vegetarian club sandwich

Serves **1**
Preparation time **7 minutes**
Cooking time **2–3 minutes**

3 slices of **granary bread**
1 **carrot**, coarsely grated
2 tablespoons **mayonnaise**
2 tablespoons **ready-made
   hummus**
1 **tomato**, thickly sliced
large handful of **rocket**
freshly ground black pepper

Lightly toast the bread in a toaster or under a preheated hot grill. Meanwhile, mix the grated carrot with the mayonnaise and season with pepper.

Spread the hummus on 1 slice of the toast and top with half the tomato slices and rocket.

Place a second slice of toast on top and spoon over the carrot mixture. Top with the remaining tomato and rocket. Place the remaining slice of toast on top and press down gently. Cut the sandwich in half or quarters and secure with cocktail sticks. Serve immediately.

For avocado, cheese & watercress club sandwich, lightly toast 3 slices of granary bread. Spread 2 slices of the bread with 1 tablespoon mayonnaise and top each with a slice of cheese, a few watercress leaves and ¼ diced avocado. Place one slice on top of the other, then top with the remaining slice of toast. Serve as above.

herby butter bean salad

Serves **4**
Preparation time **10 minutes**

2 x 400 g (13 oz) **cans judion de la granja beans** or **butter beans**, rinsed and drained
25 g (1 oz) **serrano ham**, chopped
4 **ripe tomatoes**, sliced
1 **mild Spanish onion**, sliced

Dressing
20 g (¾ oz) chopped **flat leaf parsley**
20 g (¾ oz) chopped **mint**
finely grated rind and juice of 2 **lemons**
2 tablespoons **ready-chopped garlic**
1 tablespoon **olive oil**
2 teaspoons **cider vinegar**
salt and **pepper**

Arrange the beans and ham in a serving dish with the sliced tomatoes and onion.

Make the dressing by whisking together all the ingredients. Season to taste and drizzle over the salad.

For herby chickpea & tuna salad, use 750 g (1½ lb) canned chickpeas and 175 g (6 oz) canned tuna instead of the butter beans and ham. Drain the chickpeas and tuna and toss together, then add the tomatoes and onion and divide between 4 serving dishes. Make the dressing as above and pour it over the salad.

tofu with black bean & cashews

Serves **2**
Preparation time **2 minutes**
Cooking time **8 minutes**

1 tablespoon **sunflower oil**
150 g (5 oz) **firm tofu**, cut into
   1.5 cm (¾ inch) cubes
1 teaspoon **ready-chopped**
   ginger
300 g (10 oz) **stir-fry**
   vegetables with mixed
   peppers
50 g (2 oz) **raw cashew nuts**
2 tablespoons **oyster sauce**
3 tablespoons **black bean**
   sauce
ready-cooked noodles, to
   serve

Heat the oil in a wok or large frying pan until starting to smoke, add the tofu and stir-fry over a high heat for 2 minutes until golden. Remove from the pan and keep warm.

Add the ginger, prepared vegetables and cashews to the pan and stir-fry for 5 minutes, or according to packet instructions, until the vegetables are tender and the cashews are lightly golden.

Stir in the oyster sauce and black bean sauce and return the tofu to the pan. Cook for 1 minute, then serve immediately with noodles.

For crispy tofu with ginger, chilli & sugar snaps,
toss 250 g (8 oz) diced tofu in a bowl with 1 tablespoon rice flour. Meanwhile, heat 1 tablespoon sunflower oil in a wok or nonstick frying pan, add the tofu and cook for 3–4 minutes, turning occasionally, until crisp. Remove from the pan. Add a little more oil to the pan, add 1 tablespoon ready-chopped ginger and 125 g (4 oz) sugar snaps and stir-fry for 2–3 minutes. Mix 2 tablespoons mirin with 2 tablespoons sweet chilli sauce and 1 teaspoon sesame oil and add to the pan. Remove from the heat and stir in the tofu. Serve immediately with noodles.

baby vegetables with pesto

Serves **4**
Preparation time **2 minutes**
Cooking time **8 minutes**

200 g (7 oz) **baby courgettes**,
 halved lengthways
125 g (4 oz) **baby leeks**,
 halved lengthways
150 g (5 oz) **baby carrot**s,
 halved lengthways
100 g (3½ oz) trimmed
 asparagus spears
2 tablespoons **olive oil**
2 tablespoons **lemon juice**
4 tablespoons **fresh pesto
 sauce**
salt and **pepper**
focaccia bread, to serve

Place all the vegetables in a large bowl and add the oil. Season to taste and stir gently to coat.

Heat a large griddle pan over a high heat, add half the vegetables and cook for about 2 minutes each side until lightly charred. Remove from the pan and keep warm while you cook the remaining vegetables in the same way.

Divide the vegetables between 4 serving plates, drizzle with the lemon juice, then spoon the pesto over them. Serve immediately with focaccia.

For pea & pesto soup, place 750 ml (1¼ pints) boiling vegetable stock in a large saucepan. Add 450 g (14½ oz) frozen peas and simmer for 5 minutes until tender. Use a hand-held blender or food processor to blend the soup until smooth. Return to the pan, stir in 2 tablespoons crème fraîche and 2 tablespoons fresh pesto sauce. Heat through, season to taste and serve immediately with crusty bread.

moroccan vegetable couscous

Serves **4**
Preparation time **5 minutes**
Cooking time **5 minutes**

1 tablespoon **harissa paste**,
  plus extra to serve
finely grated rind and juice of
  1 lemon
200 g (7 oz) **couscous**
300 ml (½ pint) **boiling water**
1 tablespoon **olive oil**
500 g (1 lb) **frozen grilled**
  Mediterranean vegetables,
  such as aubergine,
  courgette, peppers and
  onions
2 **preserved lemons**, rinsed
400 g (13 oz) **can chickpeas**,
  drained and rinsed
small bunch of **fresh**
  coriander, roughly chopped
salt and **pepper**
natural yogurt, to serve

Put the harissa and lemon rind and juice in a large heatproof bowl and add the couscous and boiling water. Stir, cover and leave to stand for 5 minutes. Season to taste and fluff with a fork.

Meanwhile, heat the oil in a large frying pan, add the vegetables and stir-fry over a moderate heat for 3–4 minutes. Cut the preserved lemons into quarters, remove the flesh and discard, then roughly chop the skin.

Stir the vegetables and preserved lemon skin into the couscous with the chickpeas and coriander. Season to taste and serve warm with a spoonful of yogurt and a drizzle of harissa.

For curried vegetable couscous, place 2 teaspoons mild curry paste in a large bowl with 4 tablespoons orange juice and stir together. Add the couscous and 50 g (2 oz) dried cranberries and stir well. Add the boiling water and leave to soak as above. Cook the vegetables as above and stir into the couscous with the chickpeas and coriander. Serve with a spoonful of mango chutney.

creamy leek & butter bean gratin

Serves **4**
Preparation time **2 minutes**
Cooking time **7–8 minutes**

15 g (½ oz) **butter**
2 **leeks**, cut into 2.5 cm
　(1 inch) pieces
2 x 400 g (13 oz) **cans butter
　beans**, drained and rinsed
175 g (6 oz) **light cream
　cheese with garlic and
　herbs**
2 tablespoons **milk**
4 tablespoons **fresh white
　breadcrumbs**
2 tablespoons **freshly grated
　Parmesan cheese**
salt and **pepper**

Melt the butter in a medium saucepan, add the leeks
and cook for 3–4 minutes until softened. Stir in the
butter beans, cream cheese and milk and cook for
2 minutes until the butter beans are heated through
and the sauce is bubbling. Season to taste.

Meanwhile, mix together the breadcrumbs and cheese.

Transfer the bean mixture to a warmed ovenproof dish,
sprinkle with the breadcrumbs and cheese and cook
under a preheated hot grill for 2 minutes or until the
topping is golden. Serve immediately.

For cheesy baby leeks, heat 1 tablespoon olive oil in
a large frying pan, add 16 ready-trimmed baby leeks,
season to taste and cook for 4 minutes until starting
to turn golden. Add 200 ml (7 fl oz) double cream
and cook, stirring, until bubbling. Transfer to a warmed
ovenproof dish and sprinkle with 75 g (3 oz) grated
Gruyère cheese. Cook under a preheated hot grill for
3–4 minutes until golden. Serve with crusty bread.

ricotta-stuffed mushrooms

Serves **2**
Preparation time **1 minute**
Cooking time **8–9 minutes**

4 large **flat chestnut** or
 portobello mushrooms
2 tablespoons **garlic-infused
 olive oil**
salt and **pepper**
rocket salad, to serve

Filling
200 g (7 oz) **ricotta cheese**
12 large **basil leaves**, roughly
 chopped
finely grated rind of 1 **lemon**
25 g (1 oz) **Parmesan
 cheese**, grated
25 g (1 oz) **pine nuts**

Remove the stalks from the mushrooms and brush all over with the oil. Season to taste and place on a baking sheet, skin side up. Cook under a preheated hot grill for 5 minutes.

Meanwhile, mix all the filling ingredients in a bowl and season to taste. Turn the mushrooms over and pile the filling into the cavities, pressing it down.

Cook for a further 3–4 minutes until the filling is golden and the mushrooms are cooked through. Serve immediately with a rocket salad.

For mushroom & ricotta frittata, heat 1 tablespoon olive oil in a 20 cm (8 inch) ovenproof frying pan, add 125 g (4 oz) ready-sliced mushrooms and 1 teaspoon ready-chopped garlic and cook for 3–4 minutes. Meanwhile, beat 4 eggs with 1 tablespoon chopped parsley and season to taste. Add to the pan, stir briefly and cook without stirring over a medium heat for 3–4 minutes until almost set. Sprinkle with 50 g (2 oz) ricotta cheese and 25 g (1 oz) grated Parmesan cheese and cook under a preheated hot grill for 3 minutes until golden and set. Serve with a watercress salad.

sweet treats

salted caramel brownies

Serves **4**
Preparation time **3 minutes**
Cooking time **7 minutes**

4 **ready-made chocolate brownies**
4 scoops of **vanilla ice cream**

Salted caramel sauce
100 g (3½ oz) **unsalted butter**
75 g (3 oz) **soft brown sugar**
75 ml (3 fl oz) **golden syrup**
1 teaspoon **vanilla extract**
150 ml (¼ pint) **double cream**
½ teaspoon **coarse sea salt**

Make the sauce by placing the butter, sugar, golden syrup and vanilla in a saucepan. Bring to the boil over a medium heat, stirring continuously.

Add the cream and salt and boil for 5 minutes, stirring occasionally, until thickened. Remove from the heat and transfer to a jug.

Divide the chocolate brownies between 4 bowls and top each with a scoop of ice cream. Pour over the salted caramel sauce and serve immediately.

For banana & salted caramel sundaes, make the salted caramel sauce as above. Meanwhile, roughly chop 2 chocolate muffins and slice 4 bananas. Divide half the muffin and banana pieces between 4 sundae glasses, then top each portion with a scoop of vanilla ice cream and a drizzle of sauce. Repeat the layers, ending with a drizzle of sauce. Serve immediately.

frozen blueberry yogurt

Serves **4–6**
Preparation time **8 minutes**

400 g (13 oz) **frozen
blueberries**
2 tablespoons **icing sugar**
1 tablespoon **lemon juice**
500 ml (17 fl oz) **natural
yogurt**
4 **lemon shortbread biscuits**,
to serve

Place the frozen blueberries in a food processor with
the icing sugar and lemon juice and blend until roughly
chopped. Add the yogurt and pulse until fairly smooth,
scraping down the sides of the bowl from time to time.

Divide the mixture between 4 glass dishes and serve
with the lemon shortbread biscuits.

For frozen raspberry & vanilla yogurt, place
400 g (13 oz) frozen raspberries and 2 tablespoons
icing sugar in a food processor and blend until roughly
chopped. Add 500 ml (17 fl oz) vanilla-flavoured yogurt
and pulse until fairly smooth. Serve immediately.

pan-fried apples with calvados

Serves **2**
Preparation time **2 minutes**
Cooking time **8 minutes**

2 **red-skinned eating apples**,
   cored and cut into wedges
50 g (2 oz) **caster sugar**
25 g (1 oz) **unsalted butter**
2 tablespoons **Calvados**

To serve
crème fraîche
ground cinnamon

Toss the apples and sugar together in a bowl. Melt the butter over a low heat in a frying pan, add the apples and cook gently for 5 minutes, turning occasionally, until softened.

Increase the heat to high and cook for a further 2 minutes until the apples are starting to caramelize. Add the Calvados and carefully flambé, swirling the pan gently until the flames have gone.

Divide the apples between 2 bowls and pour over the juices from the pan. Top each portion with a spoonful of crème fraîche and a pinch of cinnamon and serve immediately.

For apple & cinnamon French toast, beat 1 egg with 3 tablespoons milk, 1 tablespoon caster sugar and ½ teaspoon ground cinnamon. Add 2 slices of brioche and thoroughly coat both sides in the egg mixture. Melt 15 g (½ oz) unsalted butter in a large frying pan and cook the bread for 2–3 minutes each side until golden. Meanwhile, gently warm 175 g (6 oz) canned apple pie filling in a small pan until it is hot. Serve the French toast topped with the warmed apple and scoops of vanilla ice cream.

chocolate banoffee pies

Serves **4**
Preparation time **5 minutes**

6 **chocolate digestive
   biscuits**, roughly crushed
400 g (13 oz) can **caramel**
2 **bananas**, sliced
150 ml (¼ pint) **extra-thick
   double cream**
50 g (2 oz) **plain dark
   chocolate**, shaved or grated

Divide the crushed biscuits between 4 tall glasses.
Spoon over the caramel and scatter the banana slices
on top.

Top each portion with a spoonful of cream and decorate
with the chocolate. Serve immediately.

For chocolate fudge sundaes, place 2 scoops of
vanilla ice cream in each of 4 tall glasses. Melt 100 g
(3½ oz) milk chocolate in a heatproof bowl set over a
saucepan of gently simmering water, then mix in
200 g (7 oz) canned caramel. Spoon the chocolate
fudge over the ice cream, then scatter with a handful
of chopped toasted hazelnuts and 1 sliced banana.
Serve immediately.

raspberry ice cream

Serves **4**
Preparation time **8 minutes**

400 g (13 oz) **frozen raspberries**
1 tablespoon **raspberry liqueur** or **lemon juice**
200 g (7 oz) **mascarpone cheese**
2 tablespoons **icing sugar**
ice cream wafers, to serve

Place the frozen raspberries in a food processor with the raspberry liqueur or lemon juice and blend until roughly chopped.

Add the mascarpone and icing sugar and blend until smooth. Serve immediately with ice cream wafers.

For raspberry & choc-chip ice cream sandwiches, make the ice cream as above. Place a scoop of ice cream on each of 4 chocolate chip cookies and place another cookie on top of each to make sandwiches. Roll the edges of the sandwiches in 50 g (2 oz) chopped pistachio nuts and serve immediately.

coffee pots

Serves **6**
Preparation time **10 minutes**

4 teaspoons **instant espresso powder**
2 tablespoons **boiling water**
250 g (8 oz) **mascarpone cheese**
3 tablespoons **icing sugar**
250 ml (8 fl oz) **whipping cream**
cocoa powder, for dusting
6 **chocolate-covered coffee beans**, to decorate
cantucci or **amaretti biscuits**, to serve

Place the espresso powder in a heatproof bowl with the boiling water, stir to dissolve and leave to cool slightly.

Place the mascarpone and icing sugar in a bowl and add the coffee. Beat using a hand-held electric whisk until smooth.

Whip the cream with a hand-held electric whisk until it forms soft peaks, then gently fold two-thirds of the cream into the coffee mixture. Divide the mixture between 6 espresso cups or small glasses, then top with the remaining cream.

Dust each portion with cocoa powder and decorate with a coffee bean. Serve immediately with the biscuits.

For cappuccino meringues, make the coffee cream as above and use to fill 6 ready-made meringue nests. Top with the remaining cream, then drizzle with a little melted dark chocolate, to serve.

banana & chocolate lollies

Serves **6**
Preparation time **7 minutes**
Cooking time **3 minutes**

125 g (4 oz) **plain dark
    chocolate**, broken into small
    pieces
2 **bananas**
sugar strands or **sprinkles**,
    to decorate

Line a baking sheet with nonstick baking paper and place in the freezer.

Melt the chocolate in a heatproof bowl set over a pan of gently simmering water, then leave to cool slightly.

Cut each banana into 3 then insert a lolly stick into the end of each piece. Dip them, one at a time, into the melted chocolate to completely cover, using a spoon if necessary. Tap off the excess chocolate.

Sprinkle the lollies with the sugar strands or sprinkles, place on the baking sheet and return to the freezer for 3–4 minutes to set.

For waffles with banana & chocolate, lightly toast 6 waffles and divide between 6 bowls. Slice 6 bananas and arrange over the top of the waffles. Pour over 300 ml (½ pint) warmed ready-made Belgian chocolate sauce and sprinkle with 25 g (1 oz) chopped hazelnuts. Serve immediately with vanilla ice cream.

muffin trifle with boozy berries

Serves **4**
Preparation time **10 minutes**

400 g (13 oz) **mixed berries**,
  such as strawberries,
  redcurrants and raspberries,
  plus extra to decorate
3 tablespoons **crème de
  cerises** or **cherry brandy**
1 tablespoon **maple syrup**
2 large **blueberry muffins**,
  sliced
150 ml (¼ pint) **double cream**

Put the fruit in a bowl with the cherry liqueur or brandy and maple syrup and crush the berries with the back of a fork until well combined.

Arrange the sliced muffins in the bottom of a glass dish and spoon the fruit on top.

Whip the cream with a hand-held electric whisk until it forms soft peaks and spoon on top of the fruit. Decorate with a few extra berries before serving.

For black forest trifle, slice 1 chocolate Swiss roll and arrange the slices in the bottom of a glass dish. Mix 400 g (13 oz) stoned black cherries with 3 tablespoons cherry brandy and 1 tablespoon maple syrup and spoon into the bowl. Whip the cream as above, adding the seeds scraped from a vanilla pod, and arrange on top of the cherries. Grate a little plain dark chocolate over the trifle before serving.

chocolate & wasabi cheesecakes

Serves **4**
Preparation time **6 minutes**
Cooking time **3 minutes**

125 g (4 oz) **white chocolate**,
  broken into small pieces,
  plus extra to decorate
4 **plain chocolate digestive
  biscuits**, crushed
150 g (5 oz) **soft cream
  cheese**
125 ml (4 fl oz) **double cream**
1–2 teaspoons **wasabi paste**

Melt the chocolate in a heatproof bowl set over a pan of gently simmering water, then leave to cool slightly. Divide the crushed biscuits between 4 glasses.

Whip the cream cheese and cream with a hand-held electric whisk for about 2 minutes until the whisk leaves a trail, then stir in the melted chocolate and wasabi paste, to taste.

Spoon the mixture into the glasses and decorate with grated chocolate. Serve immediately or chill until ready to serve.

For summer berries with white chocolate & mint, place 150 g (5 oz) white chocolate, broken into small pieces, in a small saucepan with 125 ml (4 fl oz) double cream and 1 teaspoon peppermint extract. Stir over a low heat until the chocolate has melted. Divide 450 g (14½ oz) frozen summer berries between 4 bowls, pour over the hot sauce and serve immediately.

orange & ginger brandy snaps

Serves **4**
Preparation time **10 minutes**

1 small **orange**
250 ml (8 fl oz) **double cream**
1 piece of **stem ginger**, finely
  chopped, plus **1** tablespoon
  syrup from the jar
4 **ready-made brandy snap
  baskets**

Grate the rind from half the orange using a fine grater and set aside, then remove the skin and pith. Divide the orange into segments by cutting between the membranes, working over a bowl to catch the juice.

Whip the cream and orange rind with a hand-held electric whisk until it forms soft peaks, then add 2 tablespoons of the orange juice and the ginger syrup. Stir in the chopped ginger.

Divide the cream mixture between the brandy snap baskets, then top with the orange segments. Serve immediately.

For orange & ginger salad, slice the tops and bottoms off 4 oranges, then remove the skin and pith. Cut each orange into 6 slices, reserving the juice. Finely chop 2 pieces of stem ginger. Place the reserved orange juice, the chopped ginger and 2 tablespoons of ginger syrup from the jar in a bowl and mix together. Arrange the orange slices on a large plate and drizzle with the syrup. Scatter over a few mint leaves before serving.

chocolate mint mascarpone tart

Serves **6–8**
Preparation time **6 minutes**
Cooking time **3 minutes**

200 g (7 oz) **dark chocolate with mint crisp**, broken into small pieces
150 g (5 oz) **mascarpone cheese**
100 ml (3½ fl oz) **double cream**
20 cm (8 inch) **ready-made sweet pastry case**

To serve
crème fraîche
cocoa powder
mint leaves, to decorate

Melt the chocolate in a heatproof bowl set over a pan of gently simmering water, then leave to cool slightly.

Whip the mascarpone and cream with a hand-held electric whisk until smooth and thickened. Stir in the melted chocolate until well combined, then spoon into the pastry case.

Serve in slices with spoonfuls of crème fraîche, a a dusting of cocoa and decorate with mint leaves.

For chocolate & chilli fondue, place 200 g (7 oz) chilli-flavoured dark chocolate, broken into small pieces, in a heatproof bowl with 300 ml (½ pint) double cream and 25 g (1 oz) unsalted butter. Heat gently for 5–7 minutes, stirring occasionally, until the mixture is smooth and glossy. Transfer to a fondue pot or warmed bowl and serve immediately with marshmallows and a selection of fruit, such as bananas and strawberries, for dipping.

raspberry & rosewater meringues

Serves **4**
Preparation time **10 minutes**

75 g (3 oz) **raspberries**
1 tablespoon **icing sugar**
100 ml (3½ fl oz) **double cream**
1 teaspoon **rosewater**
16 **ready-made mini meringues**
4 tablespoons **raspberry coulis**

Place the raspberries in a small bowl with the icing sugar and crush lightly with the back of a fork.

Whip the cream and rosewater with a hand-held electric whisk until it forms soft peaks, then gently fold in the crushed raspberries.

Spread some raspberry cream on the flat surface of a meringue, then sandwich together with another meringue. Repeat with the remaining meringues and cream. Serve the meringues with the raspberry coulis.

For raspberry meringue mess, lightly crush 4 ready-made meringue nests. Whip 150 ml (¼ pint) double cream with a hand-held electric whisk until it forms soft peaks. Fold in 150 ml (5 fl oz) fat-free Greek yogurt, 125 g (4 oz) raspberries, 3 tablespoons raspberry coulis and the crushed meringues. Divide between 4 glasses and decorate with a few extra raspberries.

griddled blackberry pancakes

Serves **2**
Preparation time **2 minutes**
Cooking time **8 minutes**

150 g (5 oz) **blackberries**
1 tablespoon **lemon juice**
3 tablespoons **caster sugar**
6 small **ready-made pancakes** or **Scotch pancakes**
maple syrup, to serve

Place the blackberries, lemon juice and sugar in a small saucepan. Cook over a medium heat for 4–5 minutes, stirring occasionally, until softened. Allow to cool slightly.

Meanwhile, preheat a griddle pan and cook the pancakes for 1 minute on each side until heated through.

Divide the pancakes between 2 serving plates and pour over the blackberry compôte. Drizzle with a little maple syrup and serve immediately.

For griddled pancakes with lemon mascarpone, mix 125 g (4 oz) mascarpone cheese with 2 tablespoons lemon curd. Griddle the pancakes as above and serve the warm pancakes with a spoonful of lemon mascarpone and a handful of fresh raspberries.

caipirinha lime syllabub

Serves **4**
Preparation time **10 minutes**

50 g (2 oz) **caster sugar**
finely grated rind and juice of
  2 **limes**
200 ml (7 fl oz) **double cream**
4 tablespoons **cachaça** or
  white rum
pared lime rind, to decorate
shortbread biscuits, to serve

Place the sugar, finely grated lime rind and juice in a small bowl and stir to dissolve the sugar.

Whip the cream with a hand-held electric whisk until it forms soft peaks. Slowly whisk in the cachaça or rum, then add the lime mixture. Whisk until thick and fluffy, then spoon into 4 glasses. Decorate with lime rind and serve with shortbread biscuits.

For limoncello zabaglione, place 4 egg yolks and 50 g (2 oz) caster sugar in a large heatproof bowl and whisk with a hand-held electric whisk for 2 minutes, until the mixture is pale and thick. Gradually whisk in 4 tablespoons limoncello, a tablespoon at a time. Place the bowl over a saucepan of gently simmering water and whisk for 5–7 minutes until thick and the beaters leave a trail on the surface. Pour into 4 glasses and serve immediately with amaretti biscuits.

mango & passion fruit yogurt

Serves **4**
Preparation time **10 minutes**

1 large **mango**, peeled, stoned
and chopped
750 ml (1¼ pints) **natural
yogurt**
1–2 tablespoons **agave
nectar**
1 **vanilla pod**, split in half
lengthways
4 **passion fruit**, halved
crisp biscuits, to serve

Place the mango in a food processor and blend to
a purée. Place the yogurt in a large bowl and add the
agave nectar, to taste. Scape in the seeds from the
vanilla pod and beat together until well combined.

Gently fold the mango purée into the yogurt mixture
and divide between 4 glasses. Scoop the seeds from
the passion fruit over the mango yogurt and serve
immediately with crisp biscuits.

For blackcurrant & almond yogurt, purée 250 g
(8 oz) blackcurrants as above and fold into the yogurt
with the agave nectar, according to taste, and
1 teaspoon almond essence. Spoon into tall glasses
and scatter with toasted almonds, to serve.

index

acknowledgements

Executive editor: Eleanor Maxfield
Art direction and design: Penny Stock
Photography: William Shaw
Home economy: Denise Smart
Styling: Kim Sullivan
Assistant production manager: Caroline Alberti

Photography copyright © Octopus Publishing Group
Limited/William Shaw, except the following: copyright ©
Octopus Publishing Group/Stephen Conroy 9, 13, 29,
219; Will Heap 14, 17, 87, 95, 101, 119, 169, 183;
William Lingwood 37, 43, 171; David Munns 151, 165;
Lis Parsons 19, 49, 111, 121, 137, 145, 161, 191;
William Reavell 133